Embrace Your Essence

The Self-Love Workbook for Women: Discovering Your Worth, Nurturing Inner Radiance, and Building a Foundation of Unshakeable Confidence

Sophia Evergreen

Summary

Chapter 1: Understanding Self-Love

As we journey through life, one of the most essential and yet often overlooked aspects of our well-being is the concept of self-love. Self-love forms the foundation upon which we build our happiness, resilience, and overall satisfaction with ourselves and our lives. In this chapter, we will delve deep into the meaning and significance of self-love, exploring its various dimensions and understanding how we can cultivate and nurture it to lead a more fulfilling existence.

Defining Self-Love

Self-love is a multifaceted concept that encompasses the acceptance, respect, and care we have for ourselves. It involves recognizing our worth, embracing our imperfections, and acknowledging that we deserve happiness and contentment. Self-love is not to be confused with selfishness or narcissism; rather, it is about cultivating a genuine and unconditional love for ourselves, just as we would do for someone we deeply care about.

Understanding the Importance of Self-Love

To fully appreciate the significance of self-love, we must recognize its impact on our mental, emotional, and physical well-being. When we lack self-love, we may struggle with low self-esteem, feelings of self-doubt, and a perpetual sense of unworthiness. These negative self-perceptions can lead to a variety of adverse effects on our lives, ranging from heightened stress levels to strained relationships and diminished overall satisfaction.

On the other hand, practicing self-love can result in a host of positive outcomes. It enhances our resilience, allowing us to bounce back from challenges and setbacks with greater ease. Self-love also empowers us to set healthy boundaries, enabling us to prioritize our well-being and make choices that align with our values. It promotes self-care and self-compassion, making us more gentle and forgiving towards ourselves. Overall, self-love fosters a healthy sense of self-worth, leading to increased happiness, fulfillment, and success in all aspects of life.

Cultivating Self-Love

While self-love may not come naturally to all, it is a skill that can be learned and developed over time. Here, we explore various strategies and practices to cultivate self-love:

1. Practicing self-compassion: Treating ourselves with the same kindness, understanding, and support we would offer a close friend is essential. Acknowledging our mistakes, embracing our failures as

learning opportunities, and offering ourselves empathy and forgiveness are crucial steps towards cultivating self-compassion.

2. Celebrating our strengths and achievements: Recognizing our accomplishments, big or small, is key to building self-love. By acknowledging and celebrating the positive aspects of ourselves, we reinforce our self-worth and develop a healthier self-image.

3. Building positive self-talk: Our internal dialogue greatly influences how we perceive ourselves. Shifting from self-criticism to self-encouragement and replacing negative self-talk with positive affirmations can reshape our self-perception and boost our self-love.

4. Nurturing self-care: Prioritizing self-care activities that support our well-being is fundamental to self-love. Engaging in activities that bring joy, relaxation, and rejuvenation, whether it's reading a book, taking a hot bath, or going for a walk in nature, allows us to replenish our energy and show ourselves love and care.

5. Setting boundaries: Boundaries are essential for protecting our emotional and mental well-being. Learning to say no, declining activities or relationships that drain us, and setting limits on our time and energy ensure that we prioritize ourselves and nurture self-love.

6. Surrounding ourselves with positive influences: The people we

surround ourselves with greatly impact our self-perception and self-love. Seeking out relationships and connections with individuals who uplift, support, and love us unconditionally can enhance our sense of self-worth and reinforce self-love.

7. Embracing self-acceptance: Accepting ourselves unconditionally, including our flaws and imperfections, is a vital part of self-love. Recognizing that our worth is not contingent on external validation or perfection frees us from the burden of self-judgment and allows us to embrace our authentic selves.

Understanding self-love is a fundamental building block for living a fulfilled and meaningful life. By recognizing its importance and implementing the strategies and practices outlined in this chapter, we can begin to cultivate and nurture self-love within ourselves. Remember that self-love is a journey, and it requires consistent effort and patience. As we continue to explore the remaining chapters of this book, we will delve deeper into the various aspects of self-love, empowering ourselves with the knowledge and tools to lead a life filled with love, joy, and utmost self-acceptance.

Defining Self-Love and Its Importance

In this chapter, we will explore the profound concept of self-love, its meaning, and its importance in our lives. In today's busy and demanding world, it is crucial to prioritize taking care of ourselves emotionally, mentally, and physically. Self-love is not a indulgence or a luxury; it is a necessity that empowers us to live fulfilling and meaningful lives. In this chapter, we will delve into the definition of self-love, its various aspects, and the significant role it plays in our overall well-being.

Understanding Self-Love:

What exactly is self-love? It is often misconstrued as narcissism or selfishness, but in reality, self-love goes much deeper. It is about acknowledging, accepting, and nurturing oneself; a profound sense of compassionate and unconditional love towards oneself. Self-love, in its true essence, is about understanding that we are worthy of love and care, just like anyone else.

Self-Love is Multi-Faceted:

Self-love encompasses various aspects of our lives, and it extends beyond the surface level of self-care routines. It involves accepting ourselves for who we are, with all our strengths, weaknesses, and imperfections. Self-love also involves setting healthy boundaries and saying no when necessary, without guilt or fear of rejection. Furthermore, self-love includes practicing self-compassion and forgiveness, as we are all bound to make mistakes along the journey of life.

The Importance of Self-Love:

Now that we have a basic understanding of what self-love entails, let us explore why it is so important in our lives. There are numerous reasons why developing self-love is crucial for our well-being and personal growth. Here, we will discuss some of the most profound ones:

1. Boosts Self-Esteem and Confidence:

When we love and accept ourselves unconditionally, our self-esteem and confidence naturally soar. We become aware of our personal worth and capabilities, allowing us to face challenges with courage and resilience. Self-love empowers us to believe in ourselves and pursue our dreams and aspirations, ultimately leading to a more fulfilling and successful life.

2. Nurtures Mental Health:

Self-love plays a pivotal role in nurturing our mental health. Loving oneself means prioritizing mental well-being, coping with stress, and managing emotions effectively. By practicing self-love, we develop a positive and compassionate relationship with our inner selves, which in turn helps combat anxiety, depression, and other mental health issues.

3. Fosters Healthy Relationships:

Self-love forms the foundation for healthy and fulfilling relationships with others. When we love and accept ourselves, we attract individuals who genuinely appreciate and respect us. Additionally, self-love allows us to set boundaries and identify toxic relationships, ultimately leading to healthier connections with others.

4. Promotes Physical Well-being:

Taking care of our physical bodies is an integral part of self-love. Ironically, many people neglect their health and well-being while tending to the demands of daily life. However, self-love encourages us to prioritize physical self-care, such as nourishing our bodies with healthy food, engaging in regular exercise, and getting sufficient rest. By practicing self-love, we enhance our physical vitality and longevity.

5. Cultivates Personal Fulfillment:

Self-love is the key to personal fulfillment and finding joy in life. When we love and accept ourselves, we are more likely to engage in activities that bring us happiness and fulfillment. By prioritizing our passions, hobbies, and self-expression, we can experience a sense of purpose and meaning that enriches our lives.

Nurturing Self-Love:

Having understood the importance of self-love, let us now explore various ways to cultivate and nurture this essential aspect of our lives:

1. Practice Self-Care:

Self-care is an integral part of self-love. It involves prioritizing activities that rejuvenate and replenish our energy levels. This could include engaging in hobbies we enjoy, taking regular breaks, spending time in nature, and scheduling solitude for self-reflection.

2. Challenge Limiting Beliefs:

Many of us hold onto limiting beliefs that hinder our self-love and personal growth. Recognizing and challenging these beliefs is crucial to cultivating self-love. By questioning negative self-talk and replacing it with positive affirmations, we rewire our minds to embrace self-love and self-acceptance.

3. Surround Yourself with Positive Influences:

The company we keep significantly impacts our well-being and self-perception. Surrounding ourselves with positive influences—loving and supportive friends and family—helps foster self-love. Additionally, seeking inspiration from books, podcasts, or workshops that promote self-love can be highly beneficial.

4. Gratitude Practice:

Gratitude is a powerful tool in cultivating self-love. By shifting our focus to the positives in our lives and expressing gratitude for them, we develop an appreciation for ourselves and our journey. Regularly journaling about things we are grateful for can greatly enhance our self-love and overall well-being.

5. Seek Professional Help:

Sometimes, nurturing self-love requires professional guidance. If you find yourself struggling with self-love due to deep-rooted issues or past traumas, seeking therapy or counseling might be a valuable step. Trained professionals can help you navigate the healing process and guide you towards embracing self-love.

The Connection Between Self-Love and Overall Well-being

In modern society, the concept of self-love has become increasingly recognized as an essential aspect of one's overall well-being. However, what exactly does it mean to love oneself, and how does this connection impact our mental, emotional, and physical health? In this chapter, we will explore the profound link between self-love and overall well-being, delving into the reasons why self-love is crucial, its benefits, and practical ways to cultivate self-love in our daily lives.

Understanding Self-Love

Before we delve into the connection between self-love and overall well-being, it is important to develop a comprehensive understanding of what self-love truly entails. Self-love is not merely an egotistical notion or a promotion of selfishness. Instead, it is the act of recognizing, accepting, and valuing oneself unconditionally. It involves nurturing a positive sense of self-worth, embracing our strengths, weaknesses, and imperfections while treating ourselves with kindness, compassion, and forgiveness.

The Crucial Role of Self-Love

Self-love is intricately linked to our overall well-being, impacting various areas of our lives. To comprehend this connection, let us explore the significant roles self-love plays.

1. Mental Well-being

Our mental health is significantly influenced by self-love. When we accept and love ourselves, we cultivate a positive self-image, boosting our self-confidence and self-esteem. This, in turn, aids in coping with stress, combating negative thoughts and self-doubt, and fosters resilience during challenging times. By practicing self-love, we develop a greater sense of inner peace and contentment, leading to improved mental well-being.

2. Emotional Well-being

Self-love is deeply intertwined with our emotional well-being. When we embrace ourselves with love and compassion, we are better equipped to manage our emotions effectively. Self-love allows us to acknowledge and understand our emotions without judgment, providing a solid foundation for emotional growth and self-regulation. By loving ourselves, we foster emotional stability, enhance our ability to form healthy relationships, and experience greater happiness and fulfillment in life.

3. Physical Well-being

Surprisingly, self-love also has a profound impact on our physical health. Research indicates that individuals who practice self-love tend to adopt healthier lifestyle choices, such as engaging in regular exercise, maintaining a balanced diet, and prioritizing self-care. This stems from the understanding that our bodies deserve to be nourished and cared for. Additionally, self-love reduces stress levels, lowers the risk of mental health disorders that can manifest physically, and promotes overall longevity and vitality.

Benefits of Cultivating Self-Love

Cultivating self-love can yield an array of benefits that positively impact our overall well-being. Let us explore some of these benefits:

1. Enhanced Self-Confidence: Embracing self-love allows us to recognize and appreciate our unique abilities, qualities, and achievements. As a result, our self-confidence soars, empowering us to pursue our goals and dreams fearlessly.

2. Improved Relationships: When we genuinely love ourselves, we develop healthier relationship patterns. We attract positive and supportive individuals and establish boundaries that foster respect.

By loving ourselves, we are better equipped to love and accept others as they are, fostering deeper and more fulfilling connections. 3. Resilience and Inner Strength: Self-love acts as a shield against adversity. By valuing ourselves, we develop resilience, giving us the strength to overcome obstacles and bounce back from setbacks. It enables us to navigate life's challenges with grace and poise.

4. Mental and Emotional Balance: Practicing self-love promotes emotional stability, reducing the impact of negative emotions and enhancing positive ones. It empowers us to cultivate a more peaceful and balanced mindset, allowing us to respond to life's ups and downs in a healthy and constructive manner.

Cultivating Self-Love in Daily Life

Now that we have explored the significance and benefits of self-love, it is crucial to understand how we can cultivate it in our daily lives. While it may seem challenging at first, adopting these practical strategies can help us nurture our self-love:

1. Practice Self-Compassion: Treat yourself with kindness and compassion, just as you would treat a dear friend. Embrace imperfections and mistakes as opportunities for growth rather than sources of self-criticism.

2. Prioritize Self-Care: Dedicate time each day to activities that bring

you joy and nourish your mind, body, and soul. This could include engaging in hobbies, practicing mindfulness, taking baths, or seeking professional support when needed.

3. Challenge Negative Self-Talk: Become aware of your inner dialogue and challenge negative self-talk. Replace self-criticism with self-affirmations and positive statements that reinforce self-love and cultivate a healthier mindset.

4. Set Healthy Boundaries: Learn to say no when necessary and establish boundaries that protect your mental and emotional well-being. Respect your needs and prioritize self-care without guilt or fear of disappointing others.

5. Surround Yourself with Positive Influences: Surround yourself with individuals who celebrate and support your self-love journey. Limit exposure to toxic relationships and seek out communities that encourage personal growth and self-acceptance.

In this chapter, we have explored the profound connection between self-love and overall well-being. We discussed the meaning of self-love, its crucial role in mental, emotional, and physical well-being, and the benefits it brings to our lives. Additionally, we outlined practical strategies to cultivate self-love in our daily lives, empowering us to nurture this essential aspect of ourselves. Remember, self-love is a lifelong journey, and by prioritizing it, we embark on a path of personal growth, happiness, and overall well-being.

Common Barriers to Self-Love

In our journey of self-discovery and personal growth, self-love is undoubtedly a crucial element. It allows us to nourish our minds, bodies, and souls and embrace our true essence. However, embracing self-love is not always an easy task. There are numerous barriers that can hinder our ability to fully love and accept ourselves just as we are. In this chapter, we will explore some of the most common barriers to self-love and provide valuable insights on how to overcome them.

1. Unrealistic Beauty Standards:

In today's society, we are bombarded with media messages that promote unrealistic beauty standards. From flawless models on magazine covers to curated images on social media, we often compare ourselves to an unattainable ideal. This constant comparison can lead to feelings of inadequacy and a lack of self-love. To overcome this barrier, it is crucial to recognize that beauty comes in all shapes, sizes, and forms. Embrace your uniqueness and celebrate your individuality. Surround yourself with positive influences that promote self-acceptance and challenge these unrealistic beauty standards.

2. Negative Self-Talk:

The way we talk to ourselves directly influences our self-love journey. Negative self-talk can be a significant barrier, as we tend to believe and internalize these thoughts. Self-criticism, self-doubt, and self-blame can create a cycle of negativity and prevent us from truly loving ourselves. To overcome this barrier, it is essential to practice self-compassion and replace negative self-talk with positive affirmations. Treat yourself with kindness, speak to yourself as you would to a dear friend, and challenge negative thoughts by focusing on your strengths and achievements.

3. Past Trauma and Insecurities:

Unresolved past traumas and deep-rooted insecurities can stand as significant barriers to self-love. These experiences, whether from childhood or adulthood, shape our perception of ourselves and our ability to embrace self-acceptance. To overcome this barrier, it is essential to seek professional help if needed, such as therapy or counseling. Working through these traumas and insecurities with the assistance of a trained professional can pave the way for healing, self-forgiveness, and ultimately self-love.

4. Comparison and Envy:

One of the biggest hindrances to self-love is the tendency to compare ourselves with others and feel envious of their achievements or qualities. Constantly measuring our worth against others can create a never-ending cycle of self-doubt and insecurity. Overcoming this barrier involves shifting our mindset from comparison to celebration. Instead of comparing ourselves with others, we should focus on our own progress and personal growth. Remember, everyone's journey is unique, and comparing your beginning to someone else's middle or end is unfair to yourself.

5. People-Pleasing and Approval-Seeking:

The desire to please others and seek approval can prevent us from truly loving ourselves. Entangling our self-worth and validation with external sources can be detrimental to our journey of self-love. Overcoming this barrier requires setting healthy boundaries, saying 'no' when necessary, and prioritizing our own happiness and wellbeing. Recognize that your worth does not depend on others' opinions of you, but rather on your ability to authentically love and accept yourself.

6. Fear of Failure and Perfectionism:

The fear of failure and the pursuit of perfection can be significant barriers to self-love. The constant need to excel in every aspect of our lives can lead to self-criticism and an inability to appreciate our efforts and achievements. To combat this barrier, it is crucial to shift our perspective on failure and embrace it as an opportunity for growth and learning. Embrace the fact that no one is perfect, including yourself, and accept that making mistakes is an inevitable part of our human experience.

7. Lack of Self-Care and Boundaries:

Neglecting our own needs and failing to set healthy boundaries can hinder our ability to cultivate self-love. When we constantly put others' needs before our own, we deplete ourselves emotionally and physically, leading to burnout and a lack of self-appreciation. Overcoming this barrier requires practicing self-care rituals, understanding our limits, and setting boundaries that honor our well-being. Prioritize self-care activities such as exercise, meditation, journaling, or engaging in hobbies that bring you joy. By doing so, you nourish your soul and strengthen your self-love.

8. Fear of Vulnerability and Rejection:

Fear of vulnerability and rejection often prevents us from embracing self-love fully. We may hide our true selves, afraid of judgment or rejection, and present a façade that conforms to societal expectations. Overcoming this barrier involves taking risks and allowing ourselves to be truly seen and heard. Embrace vulnerability as a strength rather than a weakness, for it allows genuine connections with ourselves and others. Remember, you are worthy of love and acceptance just as you are, imperfections and all.

Cultivating a Positive Self-Image

In the complex tapestry of human existence, one aspect that stands out as paramount is our perception of ourselves. A positive self-image plays a pivotal role in shaping our lives and determining our overall well-being. It not only affects our mental and emotional health but also influences our relationship with others, our professional success, and our ability to overcome challenges. In this chapter, we will delve into the importance of nurturing a positive self-image and explore practical strategies that can help us cultivate this essential attribute.

Understanding Self-Image:

To comprehend the significance of cultivating a positive self-image, it is crucial to first understand what it means. Self-image refers to how an individual perceives themselves—both internally and externally. It encompasses our thoughts, beliefs, and feelings about our own worth, capabilities, and physical appearance.

Our self-image can be influenced by a myriad of factors, including our upbringing, cultural background, societal standards, and personal experiences. From an early age, we receive messages from our surroundings and internalize them, creating a foundation for our self-perception. These messages can be positive or negative, nurturing or harmful, and significantly impact our self-esteem and overall well-being.

The Power of a Positive Self-Image:

A positive self-image holds immense power in shaping our lives. When we have a healthy perception of ourselves, we are more likely to exhibit confidence, resilience, and optimism. This, in turn, increases our capacity to pursue our goals, form enriching relationships, and navigate life's challenges with grace.

Conversely, a negative self-image can have detrimental effects on our mental and emotional health. It breeds self-doubt, anxiety, and feelings of inadequacy, impeding our personal growth and hindering our ability to create fulfilling lives.

Recognizing the Need for Change:

Cultivating a positive self-image requires self-reflection and a willingness to acknowledge the need for change. Many individuals, however, struggle with self-acceptance and find it challenging to break free from negative self-perceptions. It's important to remember that transformation takes time and effort but is well worth the journey.

Building a Foundation of Self-Acceptance:

The first step towards cultivating a positive self-image is to develop a foundation of self-acceptance. This involves embracing and appreciating our unique qualities, strengths, and imperfections. It also requires recognizing and challenging negative self-talk, which often perpetuates self-limiting beliefs.

Practicing self-compassion and acknowledging our worth can significantly impact our self-image. Journaling, affirmations, and meditation are powerful tools that can help reinforce positive self-perceptions. By fostering a kind and forgiving attitude towards ourselves, we cultivate a nurturing environment from which a positive self-image can flourish.

Embracing Personal Growth:

Embracing personal growth is a crucial component of cultivating a positive self-image. By continually expanding our knowledge, skills, and experiences, we not only enhance our sense of self-worth but also open doors to new opportunities and achievements.

Setting realistic goals and working towards them fosters a sense of accomplishment and boosts self-confidence. Celebrating small victories along the way reinforces positive self-perception and propels us towards further growth and development.

Surrounding Yourself with Positivity:

Our environment plays a vital role in shaping our self-image. Surrounding ourselves with positive influences, supportive relationships, and uplifting experiences can greatly contribute to our overall well-being and self-perception.

Choosing wisely who we allow into our lives and distancing ourselves from toxic relationships or environments is paramount. Engaging in activities that align with our values and bring us joy can significantly impact our self-image. Seeking out mentors, positive role models, and communities that uplift and inspire us can also support our journey towards a positive self-image.

Nurturing Physical Health:

Our physical well-being is intricately linked to our self-perception. Taking care of our bodies through regular exercise, proper nutrition, and sufficient rest can have a profound impact on our self-image. When we prioritize our physical health, we not only improve our overall well-being but also enhance our self-esteem and body image.

It's important to remember that the pursuit of physical health should be driven by self-compassion rather than unrealistic societal ideals. Embracing our unique qualities and focusing on self-care can help us build a positive self-image that goes beyond external appearances.

Challenging Limiting Beliefs:

Throughout our lives, we develop deep-rooted beliefs about ourselves, often based on past experiences or societal expectations. These beliefs can become limiting and detrimental to our self-image.

Challenging and reframing such beliefs is a critical step towards creating a positive self-image. By exploring the evidence behind our negative beliefs and seeking alternative perspectives, we can break free from self-imposed limitations and embrace a more empowering mindset.

Seeking Support:

Cultivating a positive self-image is not a solitary journey and seeking support from others can be immensely beneficial. Trusted friends, family members, or qualified professionals can provide guidance, encouragement, and a fresh perspective on our self-perception.

Therapy, counseling, or self-help groups can facilitate profound insights and offer tools to navigate the process of cultivating a positive self-image. Opening ourselves up to support systems allows us to gain insights into ourselves and establish healthier patterns of thinking and behaving.

Cultivating a positive self-image is a lifelong journey, one that requires ongoing dedication, self-reflection, and growth. By embracing self-acceptance, fostering personal growth, surrounding ourselves with positivity, nurturing our physical health, challenging limiting beliefs, and seeking support, we can embark on a transformative path towards a healthier self-image.

Remember, the way we perceive ourselves shapes our reality, influences our interactions with others, and determines our ability to seize opportunities and overcome obstacles. By committing to cultivating a positive self-image, we unlock the door to a life filled with joy, success, and inner fulfillment.

Chapter 2: Discovering Your Inner Essence

In this chapter, we embark on a profound journey of self-discovery, exploring the depths of our innermost being to uncover our true essence. Our inner essence is the core of who we are, the very essence that makes each of us unique and special. When we tap into this essence, we unlock the door to living a more fulfilling and authentic life. Join me as we delve into the exploration of our inner selves and discover the wonders that lie within.

The Call of Self-Reflection

As human beings, we often find ourselves caught up in the chaos and busyness of everyday life, rarely taking the time to pause and reflect on who we truly are. We are constantly bombarded with external influences that shape our beliefs, values, and desires, often leading us astray from our authentic selves. However, the call for self-reflection resounds within each one of us, urging us to find solace in our inner world.

To embark on this journey, we must give ourselves permission to explore our thoughts, emotions, and experiences without judgment. Self-reflection is not an easy task; it requires vulnerability and a willingness to confront our deepest fears and desires. Yet, through this process, we gain a deeper understanding of ourselves and open the doors to self-discovery.

Shedding the Masks

As we delve into self-reflection, we start peeling away the layers of masks we wear to fit into societal norms and expectations. These masks often hide our true essence, making it difficult for us to connect with our authentic selves. Removing these masks can be a challenging process, as it means confronting our vulnerabilities and facing our fears.

However, it is important to recognize that the masks we wear do not define us. They only serve to protect us from judgment and rejection. As we shed these masks, we allow our true essence to emerge, like a blossoming flower, radiating its unique beauty and authenticity. Embracing our vulnerability and embracing our authentic selves is the first step towards discovering our inner essence.

The Power of Self-Awareness

Self-awareness is an integral component of discovering our inner essence. It is the ability to observe and understand our thoughts, emotions, and behaviors without attachment or judgment. Through self-awareness, we gain insight into patterns and beliefs that may be holding us back from living our most authentic lives.

One powerful tool for cultivating self-awareness is mindfulness. By practicing mindfulness, we learn to be fully present in the moment, observing our thoughts and emotions as they arise, without getting entangled in them. This practice allows us to detach from the stories we tell ourselves, freeing us from the limitations imposed by our past experiences and conditioning.

Acceptance and Self-Compassion

As we uncover our inner essence, it is essential to cultivate acceptance and self-compassion along the way. We must learn to embrace every part of ourselves, including our flaws and imperfections, with love and kindness. Acceptance does not mean resignation; it means acknowledging and honoring the truth of who we are.

Self-compassion is the natural extension of acceptance. It allows us to hold ourselves with gentleness and understanding as we navigate the challenges and triumphs on our journey of self-discovery. Self-compassion gives us the courage to face our inner demons, heal our wounds, and embrace our authentic selves with open hearts and minds.

Connecting with Our Passions and Purpose

As we delve deeper into self-discovery, we uncover our passions and purpose in life. Our passions are the fire that ignites our souls, bringing us joy, enthusiasm, and a sense of fulfillment. When we engage in activities that align with our passions, we enter a state of flow, losing track of time and immersing ourselves fully in the present moment.

Discovering our life's purpose is a lifelong journey that evolves and unfolds as we grow and change. It is the deep knowing that we are here for a reason, that our unique gifts and talents are meant to be shared with the world. Living in alignment with our purpose brings a sense of meaning and fulfillment, allowing us to make a positive impact on the lives of others.

The Journey of Self-Discovery

Embarking on the journey of self-discovery is a transformative experience that takes time, patience, and dedication. It is a journey that requires us to dive deep into the recesses of our souls, unearthing hidden treasures and confronting our deepest fears. Yet, it is in this process that we find the courage to live authentically and share our true essence with the world.

As we conclude this chapter, I invite you to reflect upon your own journey of self-discovery. What lies beneath the layers of masks you wear? What passions and purpose lie dormant, waiting to be explored? Embrace the call of self-reflection, for it is through this exploration that we find the fulfillment, joy, and authenticity that come from connecting with our inner essence.

The journey of self-discovery is not a destination but a lifelong process. In the chapters to come, we will continue our exploration, delving deeper into the intricacies of our inner selves, and unraveling the mysteries that make us essentially human. Open your heart, dare to be vulnerable, and discover the wonders that lie within.

Exploring Your Core Values and Beliefs

"What are your core values and beliefs?" This is a question that often catches us off guard, leaving us pondering our response. Many of us have never taken the time to truly explore and define the foundational principles that guide our lives. Our values and beliefs shape who we are and the choices we make. Understanding them is crucial for personal growth and fulfillment. In this chapter, we will embark on a journey of self-discovery, diving deep into the depths of our core values and beliefs.

Defining Core Values and Beliefs:

Before delving into the exploration of our values and beliefs, it is vital to understand their definitions. Core values are the fundamental principles that define what is most important to us. These principles govern our behavior, attitudes, and decisions. They guide our actions, acting as our moral compass.

On the other hand, beliefs are the thoughts, opinions, or convictions we hold about the world, ourselves, and others. They are formed through our experiences, upbringing, and societal influences. Beliefs shape our perspectives and lay the groundwork for our values.

Exploration through Reflection:

To truly uncover our core values and beliefs, we must embark on a journey of self-reflection. Carving out dedicated time and space to sit with our thoughts and emotions is essential. Engaging in practices like meditation, journaling, or simply taking a long walk alone can help us tap into our inner selves.

1. Reflect on your upbringing: Our upbringing plays a significant role in shaping our beliefs and values. Consider the values that were instilled in you during childhood. How have they shaped your current beliefs and values? Were there any significant events or experiences that influenced your perspective?

2. Identify influential figures: Think about the people who have had a profound impact on your life. These could be family members, mentors, or even historical figures. What qualities or beliefs did they possess that resonated with you? Have these influenced your own values and beliefs?

3. Explore your passions and interests: Your passions and interests can provide valuable insight into your core values and beliefs. What activities or causes ignite a fire within you? Why do these particular things matter to you? Understanding what truly matters to you can help uncover your values.

4. Observe your emotions: Our emotions often point to what we
genuinely care about. Pay attention to the things that make you
happy, angry, or sad. These emotions can guide you towards your
deeply held values and beliefs.

5. Question your assumptions: Challenge your assumptions and
opinions about various aspects of life. Ask yourself why you hold
certain beliefs and whether they align with your values. It's essential
to detach from preconceived notions and open yourself up to new
perspectives.

Analyzing and Prioritizing:

Once you have gathered insights through self-reflection, it's time to
analyze and prioritize your core values and beliefs. Creating a list of
your values and beliefs can help bring clarity to your thought
process. Here's how you can proceed:

1. Write down your values: Start by listing out the values that are
most important to you. This could include integrity, honesty,
freedom, respect, or compassion, among others. Don't worry about
the number of values on your list at this stage.

2. Reflect on the origins: For each value, reflect on why it is
important to you. Consider the experiences or influences that have
contributed to its significance in your life. This reflection will help

you gain a deeper understanding of why certain values resonate with you more than others.

3. Evaluate consistency: Next, evaluate the consistency between your values and your day-to-day actions. Are you truly living in alignment with your values? If not, why? Identifying any discrepancies can provide an opportunity for personal growth and change.

4. Prioritize your values: Once you have analyzed your values, consider prioritizing them. Which values are non-negotiable for you? Which ones hold the most weight in guiding your decisions? Prioritization can help you make clearer, more intentional choices aligned with your core values.

Living Authentically:

Understanding and embracing our core values and beliefs empowers us to live authentically. When we align our actions with our values, we experience a sense of purpose, satisfaction, and fulfillment. Here are a few tips to help you live in harmony with your values:

1. Regularly revisit and reassess: As you grow and evolve, your values and beliefs may shift. Regularly revisit and reassess your core values to ensure they reflect who you are at each stage of your journey. Adjustments are natural, and embracing change is part of living an authentic life.

2. Be intentional: Mindfully integrate your values into your daily life. Pause and reflect before making decisions to ensure they align with your values. By living intentionally, you can avoid regret and cultivate a life that is in harmony with your deepest beliefs.

3. Surround yourself with like-minded individuals: Seek out communities and individuals who share your core values. Surrounding yourself with like-minded people provides a strong support system and encourages growth and personal development.

4. Embrace growth opportunities: Stepping outside of our comfort zones allows us to challenge our beliefs and expand our horizons. Embrace growth opportunities that may challenge your values, as they can lead to deeper understanding and personal development.

Exploring our core values and beliefs is an ongoing journey. It requires us to constantly question, reflect, and reassess who we are and what truly matters in our lives. By engaging in this exploration, we gain clarity, purpose, and the ability to live authentically. Understanding our values and beliefs enables us to make conscious choices and create a life that aligns with our deepest convictions. So, dive deep into the depths of your being, explore your core values, and embark on the path of self-discovery and personal growth.

Unearthing Your Passions and Talents

Imagine waking up every morning bursting with enthusiasm, eager to dive into a day filled with activities you're truly passionate about. Picture feeling a deep sense of fulfillment as you utilize your unique talents and make meaningful contributions to the world. This is the power of discovering your passions and unearthing your talents. In this chapter, we will embark on a journey of self-discovery, delving into the depths of our being, and unlocking the hidden treasures that lie within.

Understanding Passions: Fuel for the Soul

Passions are the fuel that ignites our souls, the driving force behind our actions and accomplishments. They are the activities that fill us with joy, purpose, and boundless energy. However, identifying our passions can be an elusive task. It requires a deep exploration of our true desires and a willingness to look beyond societal expectations.

To unearth your passions, start by paying attention to the activities that uplift you, invigorate you, and make time fly. Reflect upon moments when you feel completely engrossed and at your best. These are likely the areas where your passions lie. Whether it's painting, writing, gardening, or organizing, honor these callings and grant them space to thrive.

Discovering Talents: Unleashing Your Inner Genius

Talents are the unique gifts and abilities bestowed upon us, the innate skills that make us exceptional in certain areas. They are those aspects in which we effortlessly excel, often surprising ourselves with our natural abilities. Identifying our talents requires us to observe patterns and take note of activities where we consistently outshine others.

Consider the skills that others praise you for, the tasks that come naturally to you yet appear challenging to others. Reflect on the areas where you experience flow and achieve outstanding results effortlessly. These are indications of your talents; embrace them, nurture them, and cultivate them further.

Embracing Curiosity: The Gateway to Passion

Curiosity is the gateway to unearthing our passions and talents. It is the childlike wonder that propels us into new realms of exploration, opening doors we never knew existed. Cultivating curiosity means adopting a mindset of perpetual learning and seeking out novel experiences.

Take time to reflect on your interests, ask probing questions, and embark on new adventures. Engage in activities that pique your curiosity, step outside your comfort zone, and explore unfamiliar domains. By nurturing your curiosity, you create ample opportunities for new passions and talents to emerge.

Overcoming Limiting Beliefs: A Barrier to Unearthing

As we embark on the journey of unearthing our passions and talents, we may encounter various limiting beliefs that hinder our progress. These beliefs are often rooted in fears, self-doubt, and societal conditioning. Recognizing and overcoming them is crucial to liberating our true potential.

Challenge the belief that passions and talents must align with conventional notions of success. Embrace the notion that everyone's path is unique and that pursuing your true passions is the ultimate success in itself. Surround yourself with supportive individuals who encourage your growth and discard the opinions of those who stifle your progress.

Embracing Failure: A Stepping Stone to Growth

When on the path of unearthing our passions and talents, failure is inevitable. Embracing failure as a stepping stone to growth is vital to unlocking our true potential. Mistakes and setbacks teach us valuable lessons, refine our skills, and guide us towards a deeper understanding of ourselves.

Instead of viewing failure as a defeat, approach it as an opportunity to learn, grow, and adapt. Develop resilience and tenacity, realizing that setbacks are merely temporary obstacles. Each stumble brings you closer to uncovering your passions and refining your talents, helping you thrive in the face of adversity.

Creating a Passion-Focused Life: Integrate and Flourish

Once you have identified your passions and talents, it is essential to integrate them into various aspects of your life. Creating a passion-focused life means aligning your daily activities with your true desires and unique abilities.

Craft a vision for your life that encompasses your passions and talents. Set goals that allow you to dedicate time and effort to develop and further cultivate them. Seek out opportunities that leverage your skills and allow you to contribute to causes that align with your passions. Surround yourself with a supportive network that encourages and nurtures your growth.

Unearthing your passions and talents is a transformative journey that allows you to live a life filled with purpose, joy, and fulfillment. By paying attention to your true desires, embracing your unique talents, and developing a curiosity-driven approach to life, you unlock hidden potential within yourself. Overcoming limiting beliefs, embracing failure, and creating a passion-focused life are crucial steps on this profoundly enriching expedition. So, go forth fearlessly, for within you lies a universe of untapped possibilities waiting to be discovered.

Embracing Your Flaws and Imperfections

In a world that often seems obsessed with perfection, it can be challenging to embrace our flaws and imperfections. Society bombards us with images of flawless bodies, flawless relationships, and flawless lives. We are constantly reminded of our flaws and pushed towards seeking ways to correct them. But what if we shifted our perspective and learned to embrace our flaws instead?

Defining Flaws and Imperfections:

Before we delve deeper into the notion of embracing our flaws, let us first define what flaws and imperfections truly mean. Flaws are the inherent defects or weaknesses that exist within us. They encompass everything from physical features we perceive as unappealing to personality traits we consider undesirable. Imperfections, on the other hand, refer to the natural and unavoidable aspects of being human that make us unique and fallible.

Embracing Your Flaws:

Acknowledging and accepting our flaws is the first step towards embracing them. Society often conditions us to see flaws as something negative, but the truth is, they make us who we are. Each flaw we possess is a part of our individuality and contributes to our personal growth. Instead of focusing on hiding or trying to fix our flaws, it is crucial to recognize them as opportunities for self-improvement and self-acceptance.

Acceptance and Self-Love:

Acceptance, coupled with self-love, is the key to embracing our flaws. We must remember that perfection is an unattainable ideal perpetuated by societal pressure. By accepting our flaws, we can free ourselves from the burden of constantly striving for an impossible standard of flawlessness. Embracing our imperfections brings forth a sense of liberation, allowing us to love ourselves genuinely and authentically.

Understanding the Origin of Flaws:

To truly embrace our flaws, we must understand their origins. Flaws can arise from a myriad of influences, including societal expectations, personal experiences, and the internalization of external judgments. It is essential to assess whether our perception of flaws is based on our own genuine feelings or the judgment of others. By studying the sources of our insecurities, we can gain insight into how and why our flaws affect us, enabling us to approach them with empathy and understanding.

Shifting Perspectives:

Perception plays a significant role in our ability to embrace our flaws. How we perceive our flaws can either hinder or empower us on our journey towards self-acceptance. Instead of viewing our flaws as limitations, we can reframe them as opportunities for growth. For instance, a perceived flaw in public speaking skills can be reframed as a chance to develop confidence and communication abilities. It is through these shifts in perspective that we transform our flaws into strengths.

The Power of Vulnerability:

Vulnerability is often seen as a weakness, but it is in fact a powerful tool for growth and connection. Embracing our flaws requires vulnerability, as we must confront and expose the aspects of ourselves we deem imperfect. When we allow ourselves to be vulnerable, we open the door to self-discovery and personal development. By sharing our flaws with others, we not only foster more meaningful relationships but also encourage others to embrace their own imperfections.

Overcoming Fear of Judgment:

An underlying fear of judgment often prevents us from embracing our flaws. We worry about how society, friends, or family may perceive us if we reveal our true selves. However, in reality, the fear of judgment is often more significant than the actual judgment itself. By realizing that the opinions of others do not define us, we can break free from this fear and authentically embrace our flaws without seeking external validation.

Redefining Beauty:

One area where embracing flaws can have a profound impact is in challenging society's narrow definition of beauty. We are bombarded by unrealistic beauty standards through media and advertising, which can erode our self-esteem and perpetuate feelings of inadequacy. By embracing our unique flaws, we are challenging the status quo and emphasizing that beauty exists in diversity. It is through this redefinition of beauty that we can cultivate a more inclusive and accepting society.

Embracing our flaws and imperfections is a transformative journey that requires self-reflection, self-love, and vulnerability. As we learn to accept our flaws as a part of who we are, we unlock the power to live authentically and wholeheartedly. Rather than striving for perfection, we can embrace our uniqueness and allow our flaws to shape us into the best versions of ourselves. Remember, no one is flawless, and in our flaws, we find beauty, growth, and connection.

Recognizing Your Unique Beauty

When we look in the mirror, it is all too easy to focus on our perceived flaws and imperfections. We compare ourselves to the airbrushed images in magazines or the seemingly perfect lives of others on social media. In a world that constantly reinforces unrealistic beauty standards, it is crucial to remember that each of us possesses a unique beauty that cannot be replicated. This chapter aims to help you recognize and embrace your individuality and to celebrate the beauty that is distinctly yours.

Understanding Beauty:

Before we delve further into recognizing our unique beauty, it is essential to redefine and challenge our understanding of what beauty truly is. The concept of beauty has been commodified and centered around physical appearance for far too long. However, beauty is not limited to a particular body type, facial structure, or skin color.

True beauty encompasses our authentic selves—the inner qualities, personality, and experiences that shape us. It is the self-assurance that radiates from within and the genuine smile that reaches our eyes. Embracing our unique beauty requires accepting our flaws, exploring our passions, and being unapologetically ourselves.

The Power of Self-Acceptance:

Recognizing our unique beauty starts with self-acceptance. Society bombards us with messages that we are not enough, that we should strive for flawlessness, and that we need to conform to certain ideals. However, the truth is that these standards are unrealistic and unattainable.

Embracing self-acceptance means acknowledging our strengths, accepting our limitations, and loving ourselves unconditionally. It is about understanding that real beauty lies in our ability to be authentic and compassionate towards ourselves and others. By embracing self-acceptance, we create a foundation upon which our unique beauty can flourish.

Uncovering Your Inner Beauty:

Our unique beauty is hidden within the depths of our souls, waiting to be discovered and shared with the world. To recognize and appreciate it fully, we must embark on a journey of self-discovery. This journey involves exploring our passions, nurturing our talents, and accepting all aspects of ourselves.

By engaging in activities that bring us joy, we unleash our creative potential and tap into our inner beauty. Whether it be painting, dancing, writing, or cooking, our passions are a gateway to expressing our authentic selves. When we allow ourselves to be immersed in what we love, we radiate a unique beauty that captivates those around us.

Embracing Imperfections:

We live in a world that often promotes an unrealistic standard of perfection. However, it is imperfections that make us human and, ultimately, beautiful. Each scar, freckle, or wrinkle tells a story of resilience, growth, and lived experiences.

Embracing our imperfections is not about resigning to them but rather reframing them as unique attributes that define us. Society may label them as flaws, but we have the power to redefine their significance. Embracing our imperfections means accepting ourselves wholly, acknowledging that we are a work in progress, and celebrating the beauty that lies within our flaws.

Honoring Diversity:

A crucial aspect of recognizing our unique beauty is acknowledging and celebrating the diversity that exists around us. Each individual is a masterpiece, rich in cultural heritage, life experiences, and personal stories. By embracing diversity, we create a world where different forms of beauty are equally valued and appreciated.

Let us challenge societal beauty norms that perpetuate discrimination and marginalization. By rejecting narrow definitions of beauty, we open ourselves up to a world of awe-inspiring diversity. Recognizing beauty in others amplifies our ability to recognize and appreciate our unique beauty.

The Beauty of Connection:

As humans, we possess an innate desire for connection and belonging. Recognizing our unique beauty can deepen our connections with others, fostering a sense of belonging and enhancing our overall well-being. When we embrace our authentic selves, we radiate positive energy that attracts like-minded individuals into our lives.

Meaningful relationships that acknowledge and celebrate our unique beauty provide a powerful support system. Surrounding ourselves with people who recognize our individual strengths and encourage our personal growth creates a space for our beauty to bloom. Recognizing your unique beauty is an ongoing journey, filled with self-reflection, self-acceptance, and self-love. By understanding that beauty is not confined to societal expectations, embracing our imperfections, nurturing our passions, and celebrating diversity, we embark on a path towards greater authenticity and fulfillment.

Let us liberate ourselves from the shackles of unrealistic beauty standards and embrace the beauty that is distinctly ours. Each one of us possesses a unique beauty that the world eagerly awaits to see. Remember, your beauty is extraordinary, your beauty is priceless, and your beauty is unmatched.

Chapter 3: Nurturing Self-Care Practices

In the fast-paced world we live in today, taking care of ourselves often takes a backseat in our priorities. Our lives are filled with deadlines, responsibilities, and commitments that leave us drained and overwhelmed. However, it is essential to remember that self-care is not a luxury but a necessity for maintaining our physical, mental, and emotional well-being.

In this chapter, we will explore self-care practices that can help us nurture and rejuvenate ourselves. These practices are not meant to be quick fixes but rather sustainable habits that can be incorporated into our daily lives. Remember, self-care is an ongoing journey, and it is vital to be patient and compassionate with ourselves as we navigate this process.

Understanding Self-Care

Self-care is often misunderstood and considered as indulgence or selfishness. However, it is crucial to recognize that self-care is about preserving and enhancing our overall well-being. It involves deliberately taking care of our physical, mental, and emotional health, creating a harmonious balance in our lives.

Self-care can take various forms, and it is a highly individualized practice. What works for one person may not work for another. Therefore, it is essential to explore different self-care practices and identify the ones that resonate with us personally.

Setting Boundaries

One of the fundamental aspects of self-care is setting boundaries. Boundaries help us establish limits and protect our time, energy, and emotional well-being. By setting boundaries with others, we communicate our needs and prevent ourselves from feeling overwhelmed or taken advantage of.

Setting boundaries can be challenging initially, especially if we have a habit of putting others' needs before our own. It is crucial to remember that boundaries are not selfish but necessary for our overall well-being. Start small by learning to say "no" when you feel overwhelmed or unable to fulfill a request. Gradually, you will become more comfortable with setting boundaries and taking ownership of your time and energy.

Physical Self-Care

Physical self-care involves taking care of our bodies, ensuring they are nourished, rested, and maintained. It is the foundation upon which all other forms of self-care are built. Here are some practices that can help nurture physical well-being:

1. Sleep: Getting adequate sleep is vital for our overall health. Aim for seven to nine hours of quality sleep each night. Establish a consistent bedtime routine, create a calm sleeping environment, and prioritize sleep as a non-negotiable aspect of your daily routine.

2. Nutrition: Nourishing our bodies with a balanced diet is crucial. Focus on consuming whole foods, fruits, vegetables, lean proteins, and healthy fats. Limit processed foods, sugary snacks, and excessive caffeine intake. Listen to your body and eat when you are hungry. Remember, it's about nourishing, not depriving, yourself.

3. Exercise: Engaging in regular physical activity is not only beneficial for our physical health but also for our mental and emotional well-being. Find an exercise routine that suits your preferences, whether it be jogging, yoga, dancing, or even gardening. Make it a habit and prioritize moving your body every day.

Mental and Emotional Self-Care

While physical self-care is crucial, mental and emotional well-being is equally important. Here are some practices that can help nurture your mental and emotional health:

1. Mindfulness and Meditation: Practicing mindfulness and meditation allows us to cultivate present-moment awareness, reduce stress, and enhance our overall well-being. Set aside a few minutes each day to engage in mindfulness or meditation practices. Focus on your breath, observe your thoughts without judgment, and let go of any tension or stress that you may be holding onto.

2. Emotional Expression: It is essential to honor and express our emotions. Find healthy and constructive ways to express your feelings, whether it be through journaling, talking to a trusted friend or therapist, or engaging in creative activities such as painting or playing a musical instrument. Allow yourself the space to process and release any pent-up emotions.

3. Leisure Activities: Engaging in activities that bring you joy and relaxation is vital for your mental and emotional well-being. Set aside time each week to participate in activities that recharge and rejuvenate you. It could be reading a book, taking a long bath, going for a walk in nature, or engaging in hobbies that bring you pleasure.

Relationships and Social Support

Nurturing healthy relationships and seeking social support is an essential aspect of self-care. Here are some practices to foster meaningful connections:

1. Cultivate Supportive Relationships: Surround yourself with individuals who uplift and support you. Invest time and energy into building meaningful connections with friends, family, or support groups. Engage in open and honest communication, express your needs, and reciprocate the support and love you receive.

2. Set Healthy Relationship Boundaries: Just as setting boundaries is important with yourself, it is equally important in your relationships. Establish healthy boundaries with your loved ones, communicate your needs and expectations, and ensure that the relationships in your life are nurturing rather than draining.

3. Seek Professional Help: If you are struggling with your mental or emotional well-being, do not hesitate to seek professional help. A licensed therapist or counselor can provide you with the guidance and support you need to navigate any challenges you may be facing.

In this chapter, we have explored the importance of self-care and various practices that can help nurture and rejuvenate ourselves physically, mentally, and emotionally. Remember, self-care is a personal journey, and it may take time to find the practices that work best for you. Be patient and kind to yourself as you embark on this transformative journey. By prioritizing self-care and integrating these practices into your daily life, you will be able to cultivate a profound sense of well-being and live a more balanced and fulfilling life.

The Art of Physical Self-Care

In today's fast-paced world, it's easy to get carried away by our responsibilities and neglect our own well-being. However, it is imperative that we take the time to care for ourselves physically and mentally. The art of physical self-care entails actively nurturing our bodies and minds, honoring their needs and allowing ourselves to thrive. In this chapter, we will explore various aspects of physical self-care, encompassing exercise, nutrition, sleep, and relaxation techniques. By cultivating these practices, we can enhance our overall well-being, leading to a healthier and more fulfilling life.

Section 1: Exercise for Mind and Body

Regular physical activity is not only essential for maintaining a healthy body but also for promoting mental well-being. Engaging in exercise releases endorphins, which are known as "feel-good" hormones, leading to improved mood and reduced stress levels. Ranging from cardiovascular exercises like running, swimming, or cycling to strength training and yoga, there is an exercise routine suitable for everyone. The key is finding an activity you enjoy, ensuring consistency, and gradually challenging yourself to reach new goals.

Section 2: Nourishment from Within

Eating a well-balanced diet is a fundamental aspect of physical self-care. Nutritious and wholesome food choices provide the fuel our bodies need to function optimally. Incorporating a variety of fruits, vegetables, lean proteins, whole grains, and healthy fats into our meals is crucial. Understanding portion control, hydrating adequately, and avoiding excessive processed foods are additional pillars of maintaining a healthy eating routine. By nourishing our bodies properly, we boost our energy levels, strengthen our immune system, and support our overall well-being.

Section 3: The Power of Quality Sleep

Sleep is often undervalued, yet it plays a significant role in our physical and mental health. Establishing a consistent sleep routine allows our bodies to rejuvenate, repair tissues, consolidate memory, and regulate hormones. Many factors can disrupt our sleep patterns, such as stress, excessive screen time, or an unsuitable sleeping environment. Implementing strategies like creating a relaxing bedtime routine, reducing caffeine intake, and prioritizing a comfortable sleep environment can promote restful, restorative sleep.

Section 4: Cultivating Relaxation Techniques

Amidst the chaos of daily life, it is vital to carve out time for relaxation and stress reduction. Engaging in relaxation techniques helps restore balance to our bodies and minds. Practices such as meditation, deep breathing exercises, mindfulness, and aromatherapy can soothe our nervous system, reduce anxiety, and enhance our overall well-being. These techniques can be incorporated into our daily routines, allowing us to better navigate stress and promote a sense of tranquility.

Section 5: Seeking Professional Support

Self-care also includes recognizing when to seek professional help. Our bodies and minds are complex, and sometimes professional guidance is necessary to overcome certain challenges. Consulting with healthcare professionals, therapists, or nutritionists can provide valuable insights, personalized guidance, and encouragement on our journey to physical and mental well-being. Taking this step demonstrates a commitment to self-care and an acknowledgment that assistance is sometimes essential.

Section 6: Scheduling "Me Time"

In our increasingly busy lives, it is crucial to prioritize "me time" regularly. This entails intentionally setting aside moments solely dedicated to our own self-care and rejuvenation. This could include activities such as reading a book, taking a leisurely bath, engaging in a hobby, going for a walk in nature, or simply enjoying quiet reflection. By scheduling "me time" into our calendars, we ensure that our self-care routines remain a consistent priority, allowing us to recharge and be more present in all aspects of our lives.

Section 7: Embracing Boundaries and Saying No

Implementing healthy boundaries and learning to say no are essential aspects of physical self-care. It is crucial to understand our limits and not overextend ourselves, both physically and emotionally. Saying no to activities, commitments, or situations that drain our energy or jeopardize our well-being is an act of self-respect. By setting clear boundaries, we create space for self-care and make our physical and mental health a priority.

Section 8: The Power of Gratitude and Positive Affirmations
Cultivating gratitude and positive affirmations can significantly impact our physical and mental well-being. Practicing gratitude reminds us to focus on the positive aspects of our lives, encourages a more optimistic outlook, and fosters emotional resilience. Similarly, positive affirmations help rewire our minds to embrace self-compassion, self-love, and a positive self-image. Incorporating these practices into our daily lives empowers us to view ourselves and the world through a lens of gratitude and positivity.

The art of physical self-care is an ongoing journey that requires dedication, self-awareness, and intentional choices. By actively nurturing our bodies and minds, we can cultivate a life imbued with vitality, balance, and fulfillment. Embracing exercise, nutrition, quality sleep, relaxation techniques, while seeking professional support when needed, allows us to thrive physically and mentally. Moreover, setting aside time for ourselves, embracing healthy boundaries, and fostering gratitude and positive affirmations create a solid foundation for holistic self-care. Remember, you hold the key to your well-being, and by prioritizing physical self-care, you embark on a transformative path towards a healthier, happier life.

Nourishing Your Emotional Well-being

In the fast-paced modern world, people often prioritize physical health and neglect their emotional well-being. We invest so much time and effort in taking care of our bodies, maintaining a healthy diet, and exercising regularly. While these practices are crucial for overall well-being, we must not overlook the significance of nurturing our emotional selves.

Just as we feed our bodies with nutritious food, our emotional well-being requires attention, care, and nourishment. In this chapter, we will explore various strategies and practices that can help you enhance your emotional well-being, leading to a more fulfilling and balanced life.

1. Cultivating Mindfulness:

Mindfulness is the art of being fully present in the moment, without judgment or attachment. Cultivating mindfulness allows us to observe our thoughts and emotions, and to respond rather than react. By practicing mindfulness, we create space between ourselves and our emotions, enabling us to better understand and regulate them.

One effective way to cultivate mindfulness is through meditation. Find a quiet and comfortable place to sit, close your eyes, and take a few deep breaths. Focus on the sensation of your breath entering and leaving your body. As thoughts or emotions arise, acknowledge them without judgment and gently bring your focus back to your breath. Regular meditation practice can help improve emotional regulation and overall well-being.

2. Building Emotional Intelligence:

Emotional intelligence is the ability to recognize, understand, and manage our own emotions and those of others. It enables us to navigate relationships effectively, make better decisions, and respond empathetically to different situations. Developing emotional intelligence requires self-awareness, empathy, and active listening.

Start by becoming more aware of your own emotions. Notice how you feel in different situations and reflect on the underlying reasons for those emotions. Practice active listening and empathy by engaging in meaningful conversations with friends, family, or colleagues. By actively listening to others and trying to understand their perspectives, we can build stronger connections and nurture our emotional well-being.

3. Expressing Emotions:

Suppressing emotions can have detrimental effects on our emotional well-being. It is essential to express our emotions honestly and openly, both to ourselves and to others. By doing so, we allow ourselves to process and release pent-up emotions, leading to emotional clarity and increased self-awareness.

Find healthy outlets for your emotions, such as journaling, painting, dancing, or talking to a trusted friend or therapist. Engaging in creative activities can provide an avenue for self-expression and facilitate emotional healing. Remember, emotions are a natural part of the human experience, and expressing them in healthy ways is crucial for our well-being.

4. Cultivating Positive Relationships:

Human connections serve as a vital source of emotional nourishment. Cultivating positive relationships with family, friends, and even coworkers can significantly impact our emotional well-being. It is important to surround ourselves with individuals who support, encourage, and uplift us.

Invest time and effort in building and maintaining healthy relationships. Practice active appreciation and express gratitude for the people in your life. Engage in meaningful conversations and spend quality time together. By fostering positive relationships, we create a sense of belonging and strengthen our emotional resilience.

5. Practicing Self-Care:

Self-care is often misunderstood as indulgence or selfishness. However, it is an essential practice for nurturing emotional well-being. Taking care of ourselves physically, mentally, and emotionally allows us to show up as our best selves in all aspects of life.

Incorporate self-care activities into your daily routine, such as exercise, healthy eating, and quality sleep. Engage in activities that bring you joy and relaxation, such as reading, practicing hobbies, or enjoying nature. Prioritize your needs and set boundaries to prevent burnout. Remember, self-care is not a luxury; it is a necessity for our emotional well-being.

6. Challenging Negative Thought Patterns:

Our thoughts greatly influence our emotions. Negative thought patterns, such as self-criticism and catastrophizing, can have a powerful impact on our emotional well-being. Recognizing and challenging these negative thoughts can help us maintain a positive and balanced mindset.

Start by becoming aware of any negative thought patterns that arise throughout your day. Question the validity of these thoughts and seek evidence to challenge them. Replace negative self-talk with positive and affirming statements. By consciously shifting our mindset, we can rewire our brains to focus on the positive, leading to enhanced emotional well-being.

Nurturing your emotional well-being is a lifelong journey that requires intention, practice, and self-compassion. By cultivating mindfulness, building emotional intelligence, expressing emotions, fostering positive relationships, practicing self-care, and challenging negative thought patterns, you can create a solid foundation for emotional well-being.

Remember, emotional well-being is not about never experiencing negative emotions but rather about developing resilience and coping strategies to navigate life's ups and downs. By prioritizing and nourishing your emotional well-being, you can lead a more balanced, meaningful, and fulfilling life.

Intellectual Growth and Continuous Learning

In a rapidly changing world, the importance of intellectual growth and continuous learning cannot be underestimated. As humans, we possess an innate curiosity that drives us to uncover new information, question existing knowledge, and expand our understanding of the world around us. This chapter explores the significance of intellectual growth, the benefits it brings to individuals and society, and how to cultivate a mindset of continuous learning.

The Lifelong Pursuit of Knowledge:

From the moment we are born until our last breath, we embark on a journey of lifelong learning. Unlike some other organisms, humans are not limited to the knowledge and skills they acquire during their developmental years. We have the incredible capacity for intellectual growth well beyond formal education, thanks to our ability to adapt, reason, and process complex information.

Intellectual growth involves the expansion of knowledge, the development of critical thinking skills, and the cultivation of a broad understanding of various subjects. It goes hand in hand with continuous learning, which refers to the active pursuit of new information, insights, and skills throughout one's life. These two intertwined concepts lay the foundation for personal and professional growth, fostering creativity, innovation, and adaptability in an ever-changing world.

Benefits of Intellectual Growth:

1. Enhanced Problem-Solving Abilities: Intellectual growth allows individuals to approach problems from various angles, think critically, and generate innovative solutions. This capability is particularly valuable in our increasingly complex and interconnected world, where traditional approaches may fail to address novel challenges.

2. Expanded Awareness and Understanding: Engaging in intellectual growth broadens our perspectives, increases our awareness of global issues, and develops a more comprehensive understanding of the human experience. By exploring diverse subjects and perspectives, we become active contributors to the collective knowledge of humanity.

3. Improved Adaptability: Continuous learning equips us with the skills necessary to adapt and thrive in an ever-changing society. As industries transform, new technologies emerge, and societal norms evolve, those who embrace intellectual growth are better positioned to navigate these changes and seize emerging opportunities.

4. Personal Fulfillment: Intellectual growth is inherently rewarding. Acquiring new knowledge and skills not only boosts self-confidence but also fosters a sense of fulfillment and self-actualization. As we expand our intellectual horizons, we gain a deeper understanding of ourselves and the world, leading to a more meaningful and purposeful existence.

Cultivating a Mindset of Continuous Learning:

Now that we understand the profound impact of intellectual growth, let us explore some strategies to cultivate a mindset of continuous learning.

1. Embrace Curiosity: The essence of intellectual growth lies in curiosity. Cultivate a sense of wonder about the world, ask questions, and seek answers. Treat every interaction, experience, or challenge as an opportunity to learn something new.

2. Read Widely: Reading opens the door to a wealth of knowledge and ideas. Explore diverse genres, both fiction and non-fiction, and challenge yourself to delve into unfamiliar topics. By exposing yourself to different perspectives, you'll broaden your understanding of the world.

3. Engage in Thought-Provoking Discussions: Engaging in meaningful conversations with individuals who possess different backgrounds

and perspectives can greatly stimulate your intellectual growth. Seek out thoughtful discussions, participate in book clubs, or join online forums where ideas are exchanged freely and respectfully.

4. Pursue Lifelong Learning Opportunities: Take advantage of the numerous educational opportunities available to continue learning beyond formal education. Enroll in online courses, attend workshops and conferences, or visit museums and cultural exhibitions. These activities not only expose you to new knowledge but also foster personal growth and networking.

5. Embrace Failure and Mistakes: Intellectual growth involves embracing failure and viewing it as an opportunity for learning and growth. Each mistake or setback presents a chance to reflect, adjust your approach, and develop resilience. Embrace challenges and see them as stepping stones on your continuous learning journey. Intellectual growth and continuous learning are essential for personal development, professional success, and societal progress. By prioritizing intellectual growth, we can unlock our full potential as human beings, broaden our understanding of the world, and contribute meaningfully to the betterment of society. Cultivating a mindset of continuous learning empowers us to adapt to an ever-changing world, fosters personal fulfillment, and stimulates creativity and innovation. Embrace intellectual growth, expand your horizons, and embark on a never-ending journey of discovery and self-improvement.

Spiritual and Mindfulness Practices

In today's fast-paced and hyperconnected world, we often find ourselves overwhelmed, stressed, and disconnected from our inner selves. The pursuit of spiritual and mindfulness practices has gained popularity as people seek solace, peace, and a deeper connection with themselves and the world around them. This chapter explores various spiritual and mindfulness practices and their profound benefits on our overall well-being.

Understanding Spirituality

Spirituality is a deeply personal and subjective experience that relates to our inner search for meaning, purpose, and connection. It transcends religious affiliations and is unique to each individual. It encompasses a wide range of beliefs, practices, and experiences that help individuals explore their higher self, values, and interconnectedness with others and the universe.

Although spirituality is deeply intertwined with religion for many individuals, it is important to acknowledge that spirituality can exist independently of any religious framework. Spirituality is a more inclusive term that recognizes the diverse ways in which individuals connect with their inner selves and the transcendent.

Meditation: Gateway to the Inner Self

One of the most potent practices in the realm of spirituality and mindfulness is meditation. Meditation is an ancient technique that focuses on training the mind to achieve a state of deep relaxation and heightened awareness. It allows individuals to cultivate mindfulness and explore their inner landscape.

Meditation comes in various forms, such as focused attention meditation, loving-kindness meditation, transcendental meditation, and mindfulness meditation. Each style emphasizes different aspects of the practice, but all share a common goal: to quiet the mind, enhance self-awareness, and achieve a state of inner peace.

Mindfulness: Living in the Present Moment

Mindfulness is a core concept that traverses spiritual and secular domains alike. It is the practice of intentionally bringing one's attention into the present moment without judgment. By cultivating mindfulness, individuals learn to fully engage with their experiences, thoughts, and emotions without clinging or pushing them away. Mindfulness can be practiced in many aspects of daily life, from eating mindfully to walking mindfully. It encourages individuals to observe and accept each passing moment as it unfolds, allowing for a deeper connection to oneself, others, and the world around them.

Gratitude: A Gateway to Happiness

Expressing gratitude is a powerful spiritual practice that opens our hearts and minds to the abundance and blessings present in our lives. Gratitude enables individuals to shift their focus from what they lack to what they have, fostering a sense of contentment and fulfillment.

Engaging in gratitude practices can be as simple as keeping a gratitude journal, writing thank-you notes, or incorporating gratitude rituals into everyday life. By actively cultivating gratitude, individuals become more attuned to the blessings that surround them, leading to increased happiness and overall well-being.

Nature Connection: Finding Serenity in the Outdoors

Spending time in nature has long been recognized as a transformative spiritual practice. In the hustle and bustle of modern life, disconnecting from technology and immersing ourselves in the natural world allows us to reconnect with our deeper selves and the awe-inspiring wonders of the universe.

Whether it's taking mindful walks in the forest, gardening, or simply observing a sunset, nature connection offers a profound sense of belonging and interconnectedness. It reminds us of our place in the web of life and nurtures our spiritual well-being.

Rituals: Sacred Acts of Meaning

Rituals have been practiced across cultures and traditions as a means to connect with the sacred, mark milestones, and honor significant life events. Rituals are intentional actions performed with reverence and symbolize our deepest values and beliefs.

From lighting candles and incense during meditation to participating in religious ceremonies, rituals provide a framework for individuals to connect with the divine, establish a sense of community, and express emotions associated with transitions and spiritual growth.

Prayer: Bridge to the Divine

Prayer is an ancient spiritual practice that provides individuals with a means to communicate with a higher power or deity. Prayer can be deeply personal, allowing individuals to express gratitude, seek guidance, find comfort, and cultivate a sense of surrender and trust in the divine.

Whether spoken, written, or silent, prayer is a powerful tool for self-reflection, spiritual connection, and finding solace in times of difficulty. It enables individuals to tap into their inner wisdom and align their intentions with a higher purpose.

Spiritual and mindfulness practices offer profound opportunities for self-discovery, personal growth, and enhanced well-being. By engaging in these practices, individuals can quiet the noise of the outside world, nurture their inner selves, and foster a greater sense of peace, purpose, and interconnectedness.

As we navigate the complexities of modern life, incorporating spiritual and mindfulness practices into our daily routines becomes all the more essential. By doing so, we can reclaim our inner peace, rediscover our true selves, and cultivate a deeper connection with the world around us. So, let us embark on this journey of self-exploration and self-transcendence, knowing that the path to spiritual fulfillment lies within our own hearts and minds.

Chapter 4: Building Unshakeable Confidence

In this section, we delve into one of the most critical aspects of personal development - building unshakeable confidence. Confidence is the foundation upon which success is built; it empowers individuals to overcome obstacles, embrace challenges, and seize opportunities. However, for many, confidence remains elusive, causing self-doubt and limiting their potential. In this chapter, we will explore various strategies and techniques to cultivate unshakeable confidence, enabling you to unleash your true potential and live a fulfilling, successful life.

Understanding Confidence

Before we embark on the journey of building unshakeable confidence, it is important to understand what confidence truly means. Confidence isn't about arrogance or self-importance. True confidence is the belief in one's abilities, skills, and worthiness. It arises from self-acceptance, acknowledging one's strengths, and having faith in one's capacity to navigate through challenges.

Confidence is not an innate trait; it can be developed, honed, and strengthened through conscious effort and practice. The key lies in understanding that confidence is not the absence of fear or self-doubt but rather the ability to act and believe in oneself despite those feelings. Therefore, building unshakeable confidence is a lifelong journey, one that requires commitment and a willingness to step out of your comfort zone.

Cultivating a Positive Mindset

One of the foundations of unshakeable confidence is a positive mindset. Our thoughts and beliefs shape our reality, so it is crucial to cultivate a positive outlook on life, ourselves, and our abilities. Negative self-talk and limiting beliefs only serve to undermine our confidence. By consciously replacing negative thoughts with positive affirmations and focusing on our strengths, we create a mental environment conducive to building confidence.

Practicing Self-Compassion

Often, lack of confidence stems from a harsh and unforgiving inner critic. To build unshakeable confidence, it is essential to practice self-compassion. Treat yourself with kindness, understanding, and forgiveness, just as you would a close friend. Embrace your flaws and mistakes as opportunities for growth rather than sources of shame. By cultivating self-compassion, you create a nurturing space within yourself, fostering confidence and self-acceptance.

Setting SMART Goals

Setting clear and attainable goals is an effective way to build confidence. When we have a roadmap to follow and a clear vision of what we want to achieve, we gain a sense of direction and purpose. It is important to ensure that our goals are SMART – specific, measurable, achievable, realistic, and time-bound. By breaking down larger goals into smaller, manageable steps, we can track our progress and celebrate our achievements along the way, reinforcing our confidence.

Embracing Failure and Learn from Setbacks

It is essential to recognize that failures and setbacks are an integral part of the journey towards building unshakeable confidence. Instead of allowing failures to dent your confidence, use them as learning opportunities. Embrace failure as a stepping stone towards success, viewing setbacks as valuable lessons that enhance your growth. By reframing failure as feedback and seeing it as a natural part of the learning process, you develop resilience and an unwavering belief in your abilities.

Developing Competence through Skill-Building

Competence breeds confidence. Building expertise in your chosen field by acquiring knowledge and developing relevant skills is crucial for cultivating unshakeable confidence. Identify the areas in which you need improvement, seek out resources such as books, courses, or mentors, and dedicate time and effort to acquire the necessary skills. As you become more competent, your confidence will naturally skyrocket, emboldening you to take on new challenges and showcase your abilities.

Expanding Your Comfort Zone

Stepping out of your comfort zone is essential for building unshakeable confidence. Growth and transformation occur outside of familiarity and routine. By consciously seeking new experiences, challenging yourself, and taking calculated risks, you expand your comfort zone and open yourself up to a world of possibilities. Pushing your boundaries builds resilience, self-belief, and ultimately, unshakeable confidence.

Surrounding Yourself with Supportive Individuals

The company we keep has a significant impact on our confidence levels. Surround yourself with individuals who support and uplift you, encouraging your growth and believing in your abilities. Avoid people who bring you down or undermine your confidence. Seek out mentors who have achieved what you aspire to, individuals who can guide and inspire you on your journey towards building unshakeable confidence.

Developing Emotional Intelligence

Emotional intelligence, the ability to understand and manage one's emotions, is a vital skill for building unshakeable confidence. Emotional intelligence enables you to navigate challenging situations, communicate effectively, and maintain healthy relationships. Self-awareness, self-regulation, empathy, and social skills are all components of emotional intelligence that contribute to bolstering confidence and improving overall well-being.

Building unshakeable confidence is a lifelong process that requires intention, commitment, and practice. By cultivating a positive mindset, practicing self-compassion, setting SMART goals, embracing failure, developing competence, expanding your comfort zone, surrounding yourself with supportive individuals, and developing emotional intelligence, you can embark on a transformative journey towards unshakeable confidence. Remember, confidence is not a destination to reach but a mindset to nurture. Embrace the journey and the personal growth it brings, and unshakeable confidence will become an inherent part of your being, empowering you to live a l.

Rewriting Your Inner Narrative

In the journey of life, we often find ourselves trapped in a web of negative thoughts and limiting beliefs. These inner narratives are like silent storytellers—crafting our perception, shaping our reality, and ultimately determining our self-worth and potential. Although these narratives may have been influenced by external factors, such as childhood experiences or societal expectations, it is within our power to rewrite them.

This chapter delves into the art of rewriting your inner narrative—an empowering process that can enable you to break free from limitations, unlock your true potential, and create a fulfilling and abundant life. Through a series of techniques and strategies, we will explore how you can reshape your inner dialogue, cultivate self-compassion, and embrace a new and empowering narrative that aligns with your dreams and aspirations.

Understanding Your Inner Narrative:

Before embarking on the journey of rewriting your inner narrative, it's essential to understand the influence it holds over your thoughts, emotions, and actions. Your inner narrative is the continuous stream of thoughts, beliefs, and stories that play out in your mind, forming the lens through which you view yourself and the world around you.

Often, our inner narrative is shaped by external influences like the opinions of others, societal norms, or even past failures. We internalize these messages, turning them into self-deprecating beliefs such as "I'm not good enough," "I always fail," or "I'll never be successful." These narratives can become deeply ingrained, stifling our sense of self-worth and motivation.

Recognizing the Power of Language:

Language is a powerful tool that not only helps us communicate with others but also shapes our internal world. The words we choose and the stories we tell ourselves greatly influence our thoughts, emotions, and behaviors. By becoming aware of your self-talk and the language you use, you can begin to rewrite your inner narrative for transformational change.

Take a moment to reflect on the words you habitually use to describe yourself and your experiences. Are they empowering or limiting? Do they promote growth or reinforce self-doubt? Identifying the language patterns that hold you back is the first step toward transforming your inner narrative.

Cultivating Self-Compassion:

To rewrite our inner narrative effectively, we must cultivate self-compassion—a deep sense of kindness and understanding towards ourselves. Many of us are our harshest critics, constantly berating ourselves for perceived failures or shortcomings. This critical voice reinforces negative beliefs and keeps us stuck in an unproductive mindset.

Practicing self-compassion involves treating ourselves with the same kindness, understanding, and support we would offer to a close friend. It requires acknowledging our humanity, embracing our imperfections, and offering ourselves love and forgiveness. By shifting from self-criticism to self-compassion, we create space for growth and transformation.

Challenging Limiting Beliefs:

To rewrite your inner narrative, you must identify and challenge the limiting beliefs that perpetuate self-doubt and hinder your personal growth. Limiting beliefs are deeply ingrained ideas or assumptions we hold about ourselves and the world. They act as mental barriers, constraining our potential and preventing us from taking risks or pursuing our dreams.

Begin by identifying the limiting beliefs that have kept you stuck and triggered self-sabotaging thoughts or behaviors. Reflect on the evidence supporting these beliefs and question their validity. Are they based on facts or merely assumptions? Can you find examples in your life that contradict these beliefs? By challenging and reframing your limiting beliefs, you can rewrite your inner narrative to reflect a more empowering reality.

Creating Empowering Affirmations:

Affirmations are powerful tools for rewriting your inner narrative and cultivating a positive mindset. They are positive statements that reflect the reality you want to create for yourself. By repeating affirmations regularly, you reprogram your subconscious mind, replacing negative beliefs with empowering ones.

Craft your affirmations carefully, ensuring they resonate with your goals and aspirations. Make them personal, specific, and in the present tense. For example, instead of saying, "I will be successful," say, "I am confident, capable, and deserving of success." Repeat your affirmations daily, preferably in front of a mirror, and embody the emotions and beliefs associated with them. Over time, these affirmations will seep into your subconscious, strengthening your new empowering narrative.

Visualizing Your Best Self:

Visualization is a powerful technique that harnesses the creative power of your mind to manifest desired outcomes. By vividly imagining yourself embodying your best self and living your ideal life, you can rewire your inner narrative to align with your aspirations.

Take a few minutes each day to visualize yourself achieving your goals, whether it's landing your dream job, having fulfilling relationships, or enjoying optimal health. Engage all your senses, imagining the sights, sounds, smells, and emotions associated with your desired reality. This practice trains your mind to recognize opportunities, make aligned decisions, and take inspired action to manifest your vision.

Embracing Growth Mindset:

An essential aspect of rewriting your inner narrative is adopting a growth mindset—an attitude that embraces challenges, values learning, and believes in the potential for growth and change. Contrary to a fixed mindset, which assumes our abilities and intelligence are static, a growth mindset sees failures as opportunities for learning and views setbacks as stepping stones toward success.

Cultivating a growth mindset involves reframing failures as valuable lessons, embracing challenges as growth opportunities, and fostering a belief in your ability to learn and develop new skills. By embracing the belief that you can improve, you create a foundation for rewriting your inner narrative to reflect empowerment, resilience, and abundance.

Rewriting your inner narrative is an ongoing process that requires patience, self-awareness, and commitment. With consistent practice, you can break free from the constraints of limiting beliefs, redefine your self-worth, and create a life that aligns with your deepest desires.

By understanding the power of language, cultivating self-compassion, challenging limiting beliefs, creating empowering affirmations, visualizing your best self, and embracing a growth mindset, you have taken significant steps toward rewriting your inner narrative.

Now, it's time to embark on this transformative journey—one that will unveil your true potential, unravel the stories that no longer serve you, and author a new narrative filled with self-belief, courage, and continual growth. May your newfound narrative guide you toward a life of joy, purpose, and fulfillment.

Setting and Achieving Empowering Goals

Setting goals is an integral part of personal and professional development. It allows individuals to establish a sense of direction and purpose while providing a roadmap to achieve their dreams. However, not all goals are created equal. Empowering goals go beyond mere aspirations; they encompass a deep understanding of one's values, strengths, and passions. In this chapter, we will explore the art of setting and achieving empowering goals, unveiling the principles and strategies that enable individuals to unleash their full potential.

Understanding Empowering Goals

Before delving into the process of setting empowering goals, it is crucial to comprehend their true essence. Empowering goals are those that align with your core values, resonate with your passions, and leverage your unique strengths. Unlike arbitrary goals, empowering goals ignite a sense of purpose within you, propelling you towards personal growth, fulfillment, and success.

The Power of Self-Reflection

To set empowering goals, one must begin with self-reflection. Take a moment to introspect and ask yourself: What truly matters to me? What brings me joy and fulfillment? By identifying your core values and acknowledging your passions, you can craft goals that are authentic and meaningful to you.

Uncover Your Strengths

Understanding your strengths is key to setting empowering goals. Reflect on your abilities, talents, and skills. Identify the areas where you excel, as these will become the foundation for your objectives. Remember, when your goals align with your strengths, you elevate your chances of success, making the journey more enjoyable and fulfilling.

The SMART Approach

The SMART approach is a popular framework for setting goals, ensuring they are specific, measurable, achievable, relevant, and time-bound. By applying this method, you can transform vague intentions into actionable plans, increase accountability, and track your progress effectively.

Specific: Clearly define what you want to achieve. Vague goals often lead to confusion and lack of focus. By setting clear objectives, you enhance your understanding of the desired outcome and develop a roadmap to get there.

Measurable: Establish tangible criteria to measure your progress. This helps you track your advancement, make necessary adjustments, and stay motivated. Measurable goals focus on numbers, percentages, or other benchmarks that provide a concrete measure of success.

Achievable: It is essential to set goals that are challenging yet attainable. While it is crucial to stretch yourself beyond your comfort zone, setting unrealistic goals can lead to frustration and disappointment. Assess your resources, skills, and commitments to ensure your goals are within reach.

Relevant: Every goal must be relevant to your aspirations and values. Ask yourself: Will this goal contribute to my long-term vision? Does it align with my passions and strengths? By verifying the relevance of your goals, you create a sense of purpose that drives your motivation and commitment.

Time-Bound: Set a deadline for your goals. Assigning a specific timeframe creates a sense of urgency and helps prioritize your efforts. Moreover, it allows you to break down your goal into smaller, manageable tasks, making them less overwhelming.

Visualizing Success

Visualization is a powerful tool that can propel you towards achieving your empowering goals. By creating a vivid mental image of yourself succeeding, you activate your subconscious mind, increase your confidence, and enhance your focus. Take a few minutes each day to visualize yourself achieving your goals. Close your eyes, imagine the sensations of success, and bask in the emotions of fulfillment. This exercise not only strengthens your belief in your abilities but also attracts opportunities and resources that align with your vision.

Creating Action Plans

Once you have identified your empowering goals, it is time to create action plans that will guide you towards their realization. Action plans outline the concrete steps needed to achieve your goals and act as a roadmap to keep you on track. Consider the following steps when developing your action plans:

1. Break it Down: Divide your goal into smaller, manageable tasks. This makes your goals less overwhelming and enhances your focus on incremental progress.

2. Prioritize: Determine which tasks need to be completed first. Prioritizing allows you to allocate resources effectively and prevents you from getting overwhelmed.

3. Set Deadlines: Assign timelines to each task within your action

plan. This cultivates a sense of urgency and accountability, enhancing productivity.

4. Find Support: Seek out mentors, friends, or communities who can support you on your journey. Surrounding yourself with like-minded individuals provides encouragement, guidance, and accountability.

5. Celebrate Milestones: Acknowledge and celebrate your achievements along the way. Milestones act as motivating factors, boosting your confidence and fueling your determination.

Continual Reflection and Adaptation

Setting goals is not a one-time activity; it requires continuous reflection and adaptation. Regularly assess your progress, adjusting your action plans as necessary. Life is filled with unexpected twists and turns, so it is important to remain flexible in your approach. Embrace setbacks as opportunities for growth, learn from your experiences, and make necessary adjustments to ensure your empowering goals align with your current reality.

Staying Motivated

Achieving empowering goals requires unwavering commitment and motivation. Here are some techniques to keep your drive alive:

1. Track Your Progress: Monitor your progress and celebrate each milestone achieved. Keep a journal or use a goal-tracking app to document your advancements, building momentum and reminding yourself of how far you have come.

2. Surround Yourself with Positivity: Surround yourself with people who uplift and inspire you. Share your goals with them, seek their support, and engage in positive and constructive conversations that fuel your motivation.

3. Practice Self-Care: Taking care of your physical, mental, and emotional well-being is crucial for maintaining motivation. Prioritize self-care activities such as exercise, meditation, and hobbies that rejuvenate and replenish your energy.

4. Visualize the Outcome: Continue visualizing yourself achieving your goals. Embrace the emotions and sensations associated with success. Revisit your mental image regularly, reinforcing your belief in your abilities and keeping your vision alive.

Setting and achieving empowering goals is an ongoing journey towards personal growth, fulfillment, and success. By aligning our goals with our core values, leveraging our strengths, and following the SMART approach, we unlock our full potential. Through self-reflection, visualization, and continuous adaptation, we can navigate the twists and turns of life while staying motivated and committed to our empowering goals. Remember, the key to unlocking your true potential lies in discovering your passions, harnessing your strengths, and crafting goals that empower you to become the best version of yourself.

Overcoming Self-Doubt and Fear of Failure

Self-doubt and fear of failure can be great impediments in our quest for personal and professional growth. They hinder our ability to take risks, make decisions, and pursue our dreams. Throughout life, we come face to face with countless situations that challenge our self-confidence and amplify our fear of failure. But what if we could identify strategies to overcome these doubts and fears? In this chapter, we will explore practical techniques and mindsets that can empower us to conquer self-doubt and combat the fear of failure, unlocking our true potential.

Understanding Self-Doubt:

Self-doubt is an all-too-familiar experience. It creeps into our minds and whispers destructive thoughts that undermine our abilities and worthiness. While self-doubt may seem like an insurmountable obstacle, it is essential to recognize that it is a natural part of being human. The key lies in understanding where these doubts stem from and how we can reframe them into catalysts for personal growth.

1. Embrace Self-Awareness:

The journey to overcoming self-doubt begins with self-awareness. Take the time to reflect on your past experiences and identify the patterns and triggers that lead to self-doubt. Were there specific situations or people that contributed to your doubts? By understanding the underlying causes, you can begin to address them head-on and take back control of your thoughts and emotions.

2. Challenge Your Inner Critic:

Our inner critic is often the driving force behind self-doubt. This critical voice amplifies our insecurities and magnifies our fear of failure. To overcome self-doubt, we must challenge and reframe this inner dialogue. Start by acknowledging your accomplishments and unique strengths. Replace negative thoughts with positive affirmations that remind you of your capabilities. Remember, your inner critic's voice is not the voice of truth; rather, it is a distorted lens through which you view yourself.

3. Master the Art of Failure:

Failure is often the breeding ground for self-doubt and fear. It heightens our insecurities, triggers negative self-talk, and paralyzes us from taking risks. However, failure is an integral part of growth and learning. By reframing failure as feedback rather than a reflection of our worth, we can diminish its power over our emotions and self-perception. Cultivate a growth mindset that embraces failure as a stepping stone toward success, and the fear of failure will gradually diminish in its intensity.

Overcoming Fear of Failure:

Fear of failure is a deeply ingrained emotion that permeates various aspects of our lives. It can prevent us from pursuing our passions, taking risks, and reaching our fullest potential. To overcome this fear, we must adopt strategies that help us confront it head-on, rather than pushing it aside or allowing it to consume us.

1. Define and Redefine Success:

One of the main reasons fear of failure persists is our skewed perception of success. Society often defines success in terms of external markers such as wealth, fame, or accolades. However, true success should be measured internally, focusing on personal growth, fulfillment, and impact. By redefining success on your own terms, you can refocus your energy on what truly matters and diminish the fear of external judgment and failure.

2. Set Realistic Goals and Celebrate Progress:

Setting unrealistic goals can intensify our fear of failure. Instead, break your larger objectives into smaller, achievable goals. Celebrate each milestone along the way, as this enhances confidence and reduces the pressure to succeed immediately. Remember, progress is not always linear, and setbacks are inevitable. Embrace them as opportunities to learn and grow, rather than sources of self-doubt and failure.

3. Surround Yourself with a Supportive Network:

Fear of failure often thrives in isolation. Building a supportive network of like-minded individuals who inspire and motivate you can be a game-changer. Allies who believe in your abilities can provide encouragement during challenging times and remind you of your strengths. Seek out mentors, coaches, or friends who can provide valuable guidance and perspective as you navigate through your personal and professional journey.

4. Take Calculated Risks:

Fear of failure often keeps us within our comfort zones, preventing us from taking risks and exploring new opportunities. To overcome this fear, it is essential to push your boundaries and take calculated risks. Conduct thorough research, develop contingency plans, and skillfully manage uncertainties. By embracing a mindset that values growth and learning over perfection, you will be more willing to step out of your comfort zone and confront your fear of failure.

Self-doubt and fear of failure can be powerful adversaries, but they are not insurmountable. By developing self-awareness, challenging our inner critic, embracing failure, defining success on our own terms, setting achievable goals, building a supportive network, and taking calculated risks, we can slowly chip away at these barriers that hinder our progress. Remember, overcoming self-doubt and fear of failure is not a one-time achievement but an ongoing pursuit. It requires patience, perseverance, and self-compassion.

The Power of Resilience and Self-Compassion

Life is an unpredictable journey filled with ups and downs, successes and failures, joys and sorrows. Sometimes, the challenges we face can seem overwhelming, leaving us feeling drained and defeated. However, within each of us lies an incredible power – the power of resilience and self-compassion. It is this power that enables us to bounce back from adversity, to find strength in our vulnerabilities, and to cultivate a deep sense of compassion for ourselves. In this chapter, we explore the profound impact that resilience and self-compassion can have on our lives, and how we can harness these qualities to navigate through the turbulent times with grace and courage.

Understanding Resilience:

Resilience is the ability to adapt and thrive in the face of adversity, setbacks, and challenging circumstances. It is not about avoiding or denying pain; rather, it is about acknowledging our struggles and finding the strength to overcome them. Resilience is not an innate quality that only a few lucky individuals possess. It is a skill that can be developed and nurtured.

One key aspect of building resilience is cultivating a growth mindset.

This involves shifting our perspective from a fixed mindset, where we believe our abilities and traits are set in stone, to a growth mindset, where we believe in our capacity for growth and change. When we face setbacks or failures, a growth mindset allows us to view them as opportunities for learning and growth, rather than as indications of our worth or potential. By reframing these experiences, we can bounce back stronger and more determined than ever before.

Another important component of resilience is developing healthy coping mechanisms. This involves finding healthy ways to manage stress, such as practicing regular exercise, getting enough sleep, and engaging in activities that bring us joy and relaxation. Resilience is not about ignoring our emotions; it is about acknowledging them, processing them, and finding healthy ways to cope with them.

The Role of Self-Compassion:

Self-compassion is the practice of treating ourselves with kindness and understanding, especially during times of difficulty or failure. It involves extending the same compassion and empathy that we would offer to a loved one to ourselves. Self-compassion is not self-pity or self-indulgence; rather, it is a powerful tool that allows us to acknowledge our pain and suffering without judgment, and to respond to ourselves with care and compassion.

Research has shown that self-compassion can have numerous benefits for our mental and emotional well-being. It helps to reduce self-criticism and self-judgment, fostering a sense of self-acceptance and self-worth. By cultivating self-compassion, we learn to be kind to ourselves, to forgive ourselves for our mistakes, and to embrace our imperfections.

Self-compassion also plays a vital role in resilience. When faced with difficult circumstances or failures, we often tend to be self-critical and harsh towards ourselves. This self-criticism only serves to amplify our pain and undermine our resilience. However, by practicing self-compassion, we can respond to ourselves with kindness and understanding, providing the emotional support and strength needed to bounce back from adversity.

Practical Strategies for Cultivating Resilience and Self-Compassion:

Now that we understand the importance of resilience and self-compassion, let us explore some practical strategies for nurturing these qualities in our lives.

1. Mindfulness: Mindfulness is the practice of being fully present and aware in the present moment, without judgment. By cultivating mindfulness, we can observe our thoughts and emotions without getting entangled in them. This allows us to respond to difficult

situations with clarity and wisdom, rather than getting caught up in negative thought patterns or emotions.

2. Positive Self-Talk: Pay attention to your inner dialogue and replace negative self-talk with positive and encouraging statements. Remind yourself that setbacks and failures are temporary and that you have the strength and resilience to overcome them. Practice affirmations that promote self-compassion and resilience, such as "I am worthy of love and compassion, especially during difficult times."

3. Seek Support: Reach out to trusted friends, family members, or professionals to share your struggles and seek support. Remember, asking for help is a sign of strength, not weakness. Surround yourself with a supportive network that can offer encouragement, guidance, and perspective during challenging times.

4. Practice Self-Care: Prioritize self-care activities that nourish your mind, body, and soul. Engage in activities that bring you joy, relaxation, and rejuvenation. Take care of your physical health through regular exercise, healthy eating, and getting enough sleep. By prioritizing self-care, you are better equipped to handle adversity and cultivate resilience.

5. Embrace Failure as a Learning Opportunity: Rather than viewing failure as a reflection of your worth or potential, see it as an opportunity for growth and learning. Treat each setback as a

stepping stone towards success. Embrace the lessons learned from failures and use them as motivation to try again, armed with newfound knowledge and resilience.

Resilience and self-compassion are powerful tools that enable us to navigate the challenges of life with grace and courage. By cultivating resilience, we learn to bounce back from adversity and view setbacks as opportunities for growth. Meanwhile, self-compassion allows us to respond to ourselves with kindness, understanding, and acceptance, fostering resilience and self-worth.

In the face of life's uncertainties, resilience and self-compassion act as guiding lights, providing the strength and clarity needed to overcome obstacles. By practicing these qualities, we unleash our true potential and discover the incredible power we hold within ourselves. So, embrace your resilience, show yourself compassion, and let these qualities guide you towards a life filled with strength, joy, and fulfillment.

Chapter 5: Cultivating Positive Relationships

In our journey through life, we come across countless individuals who leave a lasting impression on us. Some fill our lives with joy, laughter, and love, while others challenge us, push us to grow, and teach us important life lessons. These relationships, be they with family, friends, colleagues, or romantic partners, form an integral part of our well-being and happiness. In this chapter, we will explore the art of cultivating positive relationships and delve into the various aspects that contribute to fostering deep and meaningful connections with those around us.

Understanding Ourselves

Before embarking on our quest to build positive relationships, it is essential to gain a deep understanding of ourselves. The journey towards self-discovery involves untangling the intricacies of our emotions, desires, and values. Taking time for introspection allows us to identify our strengths, weaknesses, and areas where personal growth is needed. Through this process, we can enter into relationships from a place of authenticity and vulnerability, setting the stage for profound connections.

Building Trust and Communication

One of the cornerstones of any successful relationship is trust. Without trust, the foundation crumbles, leading to misunderstandings, conflicts, and ultimately, the deterioration of the bond. Cultivating trust requires consistent honesty, reliability, and respect for boundaries. Open and effective communication serves as a vital bridge for trust to flourish. Clear expression of thoughts, active listening, and empathy form the building blocks of healthy interactions. By fostering trust and communication, we create a safe space for both parties to be heard and understood, cementing the bond further.

Nurturing Empathy and Compassion

Empathy and compassion are the glue that holds our relationships together. Empathy involves stepping into another person's shoes and understanding their emotions, while compassion is the act of extending kindness and support towards others. These qualities help us bridge gaps, smooth conflicts, and create an atmosphere of understanding. By recognizing and acknowledging the feelings of others, we build a strong foundation for deeper connections, promoting mutual growth and happiness.

Creating Boundaries and Respecting Differences

In any relationship, it is crucial to establish healthy boundaries that respect both our own and the other person's needs. Boundaries serve as guidelines that protect our emotional well-being and ensure that relationships remain balanced and mutually beneficial. While setting boundaries, it is equally essential to respect the individuality and differences of those around us. Embracing diversity in opinions, beliefs, and values fosters an inclusive environment where uniqueness is celebrated, enriching the overall connection.

Nurturing Positive Vibes and Optimism

Positive energy is infectious and has the power to transform relationships. Fostering optimism and a positive outlook within ourselves spreads joy and uplifts those around us. By focusing on the good in others and expressing gratitude, we create an environment that nurtures positive emotions. Celebrating the achievements, milestones, and even the small victories in each other's lives adds a layer of warmth and support to our connections, paving the way for lifelong bonds.

Cultivating Friendship and Support

Friendships are the lifeblood of our social connections. They are the relationships that often withstand the test of time and provide immense support during both joyful and challenging moments. Nurturing friendships requires effort, care, and a willingness to be present. Regular communication, shared activities, and quality time help cultivate bonds that grow stronger over the years. True friendships are built on a foundation of trust, shared values, and unwavering support, offering a sanctuary where we can be our authentic selves.

Strengthening Family Ties

Our families shape us in profound ways and hold a special place in our hearts. However, family dynamics can be complex and challenging at times. Strengthening family ties involves a conscious effort to nurture understanding, patience, and forgiveness. By fostering open communication, actively listening to one another, and creating shared traditions, we fortify the bonds that tie us together. Family provides a sense of belonging, an unwavering support system, and a deep well of love that enhances our overall well-being.

Romantic Relationships and Intimacy

Romantic relationships offer a unique and profound connection with another individual. Love, passion, and intimacy create a bond that transcends the ordinary. Cultivating a healthy romantic relationship entails nurturing emotional intimacy, communication, trust, and shared values. Celebrating each other's individuality, actively resolving conflicts, and expressing love and affection in both words and actions are crucial components in maintaining a fulfilling and lasting relationship.

Navigating Professional Relationships

In our professional lives, we encounter a diverse range of individuals with whom we form connections that serve as the bedrock of our careers. Building professional relationships involves networking, collaboration, and demonstrating proficiency in our fields. These connections offer opportunities for mentorship, learning, and personal growth. By being dependable, valuing teamwork, and treating others with respect, we create a positive work environment where relationships can flourish, leading to greater success and fulfillment.

Cultivating positive relationships is an art that requires effort, understanding, and an open heart. By engaging in self-reflection, building trust, practicing empathy, and respecting boundaries, we lay a solid foundation for meaningful connections. Nurturing and celebrating these relationships provide us with a support system, joy, and growth throughout our lives. Whether it is familial bonds, friendships, romantic relationships, or professional connections, investing in positive relationships enriches our overall well-being, adding depth and meaning to our journey through life.

Recognizing Healthy and Toxic Relationships

As humans, our lives are deeply intertwined with relationships. Whether they are familial, romantic, or friendships, relationships play a vital role in shaping our happiness, well-being, and personal growth. However, not all relationships are created equal. Some relationships boost our confidence, nurture our growth, and bring joy to our lives, while others drain us emotionally and hinder our progress. In this chapter, we will explore the characteristics of healthy and toxic relationships, equipping you with the knowledge to recognize and navigate them more effectively.

Defining Healthy Relationships

Healthy relationships serve as a foundation for our emotional, mental, and even physical well-being. They are built on the pillars of trust, respect, communication, and support. In healthy relationships, both parties feel seen, heard, and valued. Let's delve into the fundamental characteristics of such relationships:

1. Trust: Trust is the cornerstone of healthy relationships. It is the unwavering belief that someone will act with your best interests in mind. Trust develops over time through consistent actions, honesty, and reliability. In healthy relationships, there is an inherent sense of

security and faith in each other's intentions.

2. Mutual Respect: Healthy relationships are rooted in mutual respect. Both parties recognize and appreciate each other's individuality, perspectives, and boundaries. Respect fosters an environment where both individuals feel safe expressing their thoughts, feelings, and desires without fear of judgment or ridicule.

3. Effective Communication: Open and honest communication is essential for the success of any relationship. In healthy relationships, there is a willingness to listen attentively, express thoughts and emotions without aggression or passive-aggressiveness, and find common ground when conflicts arise. Effective communication ensures misunderstandings are minimized, and concerns are addressed constructively.

4. Support and Encouragement: In healthy relationships, both individuals genuinely support and encourage each other's goals, aspirations, and personal growth. They understand that each person's success does not diminish their own but rather strengthens the bond and enriches the relationship.

5. Healthy Boundaries: Maintaining healthy boundaries is crucial in any relationship. Healthy relationships allow individuals to establish personal limits, needs, and preferences that are respected by their partner. Healthy boundaries ensure that the relationship remains

balanced, fostering a sense of autonomy and self-respect for both parties.

Recognizing Toxic Relationships

Sadly, not all relationships are healthy. Toxic relationships can suffocate our potential for growth, drain our energy, and damage our mental and emotional well-being. Understanding the characteristics of toxic relationships is crucial to identify and address them. Let's explore some red flags commonly found in toxic relationships:

1. Lack of Trust and Respect: Toxic relationships often lack trust and respect, which are the pillars of healthy connections. There may be constant suspicion, dishonesty, and disrespect, creating an atmosphere of uncertainty and tension.

2. Communication Breakdown: In toxic relationships, communication is often ineffective or completely absent. Conversation may be dominated by criticism, shouting matches, stonewalling, or manipulation. This breakdown of communication hampers conflict resolution and perpetuates a toxic cycle.

3. Control and Manipulation: Toxic relationships are characterized by one person's need for power and control over the other. Manipulation, coercion, and emotional blackmail are common strategies employed by toxic individuals to maintain dominance and

undermine their partner's autonomy.

4. Constant Criticism and Negativity: Toxic relationships are often filled with criticism, put-downs, and negativity. Instead of being supportive, toxic partners may belittle, degrade, or intentionally hurt the other person. This negative environment erodes self-esteem and creates a constant sense of anxiety and unworthiness.

5. Lack of Accountability: In toxic relationships, one or both individuals may refuse to take responsibility for their actions, conveniently shifting blame onto their partner. This pattern of deflecting accountability leads to a toxic dynamic where problems persist and resolution becomes nearly impossible.

6. Emotional and Physical Abuse: The most severe form of a toxic relationship involves emotional or physical abuse. This can manifest as verbal insults, threats, physical violence, or isolation from support networks. Such relationships pose significant risks to personal safety and require immediate intervention and support.

Navigating Relationships with Awareness

Recognizing whether a relationship is healthy or toxic is the first step towards creating positive change. However, navigating relationships with awareness requires ongoing effort and introspection. Here are some tips to help you build healthier connections and address toxic dynamics:

1. Reflect on Your Own Behavior: Start by reflecting on your own actions and mentality within the relationship. Are you fostering a healthy environment? Are there areas where you might need to improve your communication or understanding? Acknowledging and working on your own shortcomings can positively impact the dynamics of any relationship.

2. Set Clear Boundaries: Clearly define your personal boundaries and communicate them openly with your partner. Healthy boundaries ensure that your needs are respected, and they provide a framework for building a stronger relationship.

3. Seek Open Communication: Encourage open and honest communication by actively listening to your partner, expressing your thoughts and feelings calmly, and fostering a safe space for dialogue. Healthy conversations can help identify and address issues before they escalate.

4. Evaluate the Balance: Regularly evaluate the balance within your relationship. Are both individuals contributing equally? Is support and encouragement mutual? A healthy relationship is built on equality and should not be one-sided.

5. Seek Support: If you find yourself in a toxic relationship, seek

support from trusted friends, family members, or professionals. Their objective perspective can help you identify your options and develop a plan to disengage from harmful dynamics.

Recognizing and understanding the characteristics of healthy and toxic relationships is essential for maintaining our emotional well-being and personal growth. While healthy relationships provide a nurturing environment for individuals to thrive, toxic relationships can impede our progress and cause harm. By familiarizing ourselves with the signs and actively reflecting on our own behavior, we can work towards building healthier relationships and shedding toxic ones.

Remember, fostering healthy connections is a continuous journey that requires self-awareness, open communication, and a commitment to personal growth.

Boundaries and Assertive Communication

In our daily lives, we interact with people from various backgrounds, experience different situations, and face various challenges that require effective communication skills. One essential aspect of effective communication is setting and maintaining boundaries. Whether it's in personal relationships, professional environments, or social settings, setting healthy boundaries plays a fundamental role in maintaining our well-being and establishing meaningful connections with others. In this chapter, we will explore the importance of boundaries and how assertive communication can help us navigate these boundaries effectively.

Understanding Boundaries:

Boundaries are the invisible lines we create to protect ourselves emotionally, mentally, and physically. They define what is acceptable and what isn't in our relationships and interactions with others. Boundaries act as a self-care mechanism, allowing us to establish a sense of control and protect our personal space. Setting boundaries is not about being selfish or building walls; instead, it fosters healthy relationships and ensures mutual respect and understanding.

Different Types of Boundaries:

Boundaries can manifest in various forms, and it's important to recognize and understand these different types to effectively implement them in our lives. These include:

1. Physical Boundaries: These are boundaries that define our personal space and comfort levels regarding physical contact. They vary from person to person. Some may prefer hugs, while others may feel uncomfortable with any form of physical touch. Understanding and communicating our physical boundaries is crucial for maintaining personal autonomy and consent.

2. Emotional Boundaries: Emotional boundaries refer to our ability to separate our emotions from those of others. It's about taking responsibility for our own emotional well-being and not allowing others to manipulate or control our emotions. Emotional boundaries enable healthy emotional sharing while establishing limits on what we are willing to discuss and how much we can support others without compromising our own emotional health.

3. Mental Boundaries: Just as it is important to protect our physical space and emotions, mental boundaries are crucial for safeguarding our thoughts, beliefs, and intellectual autonomy. Our ideas, values, and opinions need to be respected and accepted by others. By establishing mental boundaries, we can avoid intellectual manipulation or unwanted influence.

4. Time Boundaries: Time is valuable, and setting time boundaries is

essential for managing our schedules, commitments, and priorities. It involves recognizing our limits in terms of availability and not overextending ourselves. When we establish time boundaries, we can ensure a healthy work-life balance and avoid burnout.

Importance of Assertive Communication:

Assertive communication is an approach that allows individuals to express their needs, opinions, and emotions while respecting the boundaries of others. It involves being clear, honest, and direct without being aggressive or passive. Assertive communication is crucial when setting and maintaining boundaries, as it allows us to effectively express ourselves and maintain healthy relationships.

Benefits of Assertive Communication:

1. Strengthened Self-Esteem: When we practice assertive communication, we value ourselves and our needs. This builds our self-esteem and self-confidence, as we no longer fear expressing our true thoughts and feelings.

2. Enhanced Relationship Dynamics: Assertive communication fosters healthy interactions and promotes open dialogue in relationships. By clearly expressing our boundaries, needs, and expectations, we minimize misunderstandings and conflicts, leading to stronger connections with others.

3. Reduced Stress and Anxiety: When we establish and maintain

boundaries through assertive communication, we reduce stress and anxiety caused by overcommitment or feeling undervalued. Knowing that our boundaries are being respected brings a sense of security and peace of mind.

4. Increased Personal Empowerment: Assertive communication allows us to take control of our lives and advocate for ourselves. It empowers us to make decisions that align with our values and stands up for what we believe in, gaining a sense of personal empowerment and fulfillment.

Implementing Assertive Communication for Boundaries:
1. Know Your Boundaries: Before communicating your boundaries, it is important to identify and understand them yourself. Take some time for self-reflection and determine what you are comfortable with and where your limits lie in different areas of your life.

2. Be Clear and Specific: When expressing your boundaries, ensure you are clear and specific in your communication. Use "I" statements to avoid sounding accusatory or confrontational. For example, instead of saying, "You always invade my personal space," say, "I feel uncomfortable when my personal space is invaded."

3. Practice Active Listening: Being assertive is not only about expressing yourself but also listening empathetically to others. Actively listen to their perspectives and thoughts on your

boundaries. This allows for an open conversation and a deeper understanding between both parties.

4. Use Non-Verbal Cues: Assertive communication is not solely about the words we use; our non-verbal cues also play a crucial role. Maintain eye contact, keep an open posture, and use a calm and steady tone to convey assertiveness effectively.

5. Set Consequences: In situations where your boundaries are repeatedly violated, it is important to establish consequences for such actions. Communicate these consequences clearly to ensure that others understand the implications of crossing your boundaries. This reinforces your assertive communication and ensures your boundaries are respected.

Establishing and maintaining healthy boundaries through assertive communication is an ongoing process that requires self-awareness, practice, and continuous learning. By recognizing the different types of boundaries and implementing assertive communication techniques, we can create meaningful connections, promote emotional well-being, and protect ourselves from potential harm. Remember, boundaries are not barriers; they are the essential framework that enables us to lead fulfilled and authentic lives.

Empowering Your Tribe: Surrounding Yourself with Positivity

In our journey through life, it becomes evident that the company we keep plays a significant role in shaping our thoughts, beliefs, and, ultimately, our actions. This chapter delves into the art of building a positive tribe around you, exploring the profound impact it can have on personal growth, happiness, and success. We will explore actionable strategies for seeking out, nurturing, and empowering a supportive network that will fuel your ambitions and aspirations.

Section 1: Understanding the Power of Positivity

Positive thinking is not merely a wishful mindset; it is a scientific and psychological concept embraced by experts worldwide. Grounded in research, psychological studies have shown that surrounding oneself with positive influences strengthens mental resilience, elevates self-esteem, and leads to healthier relationships. Moreover, being part of a positive tribe fosters creativity, enhances problem-solving abilities, and provides a robust support system during challenging times.

Section 2: Aligning with Positive Vibes

To attract positivity, we must first reflect this energy within ourselves. Choosing optimism and cultivating a grateful mindset helps us align with positivity and attract like-minded individuals. Start by acknowledging and celebrating your own accomplishments, however small they may be. This not only boosts self-confidence but also radiates positivity from within, making you a magnet for those who share similar vibrations.

Section 3: Identifying Toxic Influences

To craft a positive tribe, you must first recognize and distance yourself from toxic influences that drain your energy and hinder your growth. Whether it be friends, acquaintances, or even family members, take the time to evaluate how these relationships impact your mental and emotional well-being. Set boundaries, surround yourself with individuals who celebrate your successes, and let go of those who constantly bring negativity and toxicity into your life.

Section 4: Seek Out Positive Minds

Once you've cleared the path from negative influences, be intentional about seeking out positive minds to add to your tribe. Look for individuals who radiate kindness, empathy, and resilience. Attend motivational events, join interest-based clubs, engage in social activities, or even explore online communities that align with your values. By actively participating in environments that foster positivity, you increase your chances of connecting with like-minded individuals who will encourage, uplift, and inspire you.

Section 5: Nurturing Positive Relationships

Building meaningful relationships is a two-way street. Invest time and effort in nurturing bonds with individuals who amplify your energy and act as a source of inspiration. Engage in open and honest communication, offer support and encouragement when needed, and celebrate the successes of your tribe members. By fostering an environment of support and positivity, you create a safe space for growth, personal development, and empowerment.

Section 6: Embracing Diversity within Your Tribe

While seeking out like-minded individuals is important, it is equally vital to embrace diversity within your tribe. Surrounding yourself with people who come from different backgrounds, possess unique perspectives, and pursue various passions broadens your horizons and exposes you to countless opportunities for personal and cultural growth. Embracing diversity not only enriches your own experiences but also allows your tribe members to learn from each other's journeys, creating a vibrant ecosystem of empowerment.

Section 7: Paying It Forward

Once you have experienced the transformative power of surrounding yourself with positivity, it's time to pay it forward. Empowering your tribe goes beyond personal gain; it is about inspiring others to unlock their full potential. Share your knowledge, offer guidance, and be a source of motivation for those around you. By uplifting others, you create a ripple effect, fostering a community of empowered individuals who, in turn, continue the cycle of positivity and growth.

Section 8: Overcoming Challenges Together

Building a positive tribe does not guarantee a life devoid of challenges. However, when faced with adversity, a strong support system can alleviate burdens and inspire resilience. Create a space within your tribe where members can openly discuss their struggles and seek guidance without fear of judgment. By providing unwavering support during tough times, your tribe will emerge stronger, equipped to overcome any hurdle that comes their way.

Section 9: Sustaining Positivity in a Changing World

As we navigate through life, we must acknowledge that change is constant. Cultivating a positive tribe requires adaptability and an understanding that the dynamics within relationships may shift over time. Realize that individual paths may diverge, but the lasting impact of those connections remains. Embrace change, celebrate growth, and remain open to new experiences and connections that align with your evolving needs.

By surrounding yourself with positivity and empowering your tribe, you harness the incredible power of human connection to elevate your personal and professional growth. Remember that building a positive tribe is an ongoing process, and it requires intention, awareness, and occasional adjustments. As you enter into this transformative journey, keep an open heart, and welcome the beautiful opportunities that await you as you weave a vibrant tapestry of positivity and empowerment in your life.

Giving and Receiving Love in Relationships

Love is the invisible thread that weaves relationships together, forming a strong bond between individuals. It is the foundation upon which we build connections, nurturing and sustaining them throughout our lives. While love comes easily to some, many struggle to express and receive it in their relationships. In this chapter, we will explore the intricacies of giving and receiving love, understanding the importance of both aspects and how they shape our relationships.

Section 1: Understanding Love:

Love is a complex emotion that manifests itself in various ways. It goes beyond the mere presence of affection or desire and extends to a selfless commitment to the well-being of another person. Love can be characterized by qualities such as compassion, empathy, trust, and respect. Acknowledging the diverse forms love can take helps us appreciate the nuances of giving and receiving love in relationships.

Section 2: The Art of Giving Love:

To give love unconditionally is a skill that requires practice and patience. It involves being selfless and nurturing, prioritizing the needs and desires of the other person. Giving love does not mean sacrificing our own well-being, but rather striking a delicate balance that promotes growth and harmony within the relationship. It involves acts of kindness, thoughtful gestures, and emotional support that demonstrate our commitment to the other person's happiness.

Subsection 2.1: Words of Affirmation:

One of the most powerful ways to give love is through words of affirmation. Expressing appreciation, admiration, and affection to our partner strengthens the bond between us. By verbalizing our feelings, we validate the other person and make them feel cherished. Simple phrases like "I love you," "You are important to me," or "I appreciate you" can have a profound impact on our relationships.

Subsection 2.2: Acts of Service:

Acts of service are tangible expressions of love that involve going out of our way to assist and support our partner. By offering help with daily tasks, taking care of responsibilities, or surprising our loved one with small acts of kindness, we demonstrate our commitment to their well-being. The thoughtfulness and effort behind these acts foster a sense of security and appreciation within the relationship.

Subsection 2.3: Quality Time:

Spending quality time with our partner is a powerful way to give love. Giving undivided attention, actively listening, and engaging in meaningful conversations help establish a deep emotional connection. It allows us to understand our partner's fears, dreams, and aspirations, fostering intimacy and fostering a sense of belonging in the relationship.

Section 3: The Grace of Receiving Love:

While giving love holds immense value, so too does the grace of receiving love. Many individuals struggle with accepting love and affection due to various reasons such as fear of vulnerability, feelings of unworthiness, or a belief that they must always be self-sufficient. Yet, receiving love is vital for the well-being of both individuals in a relationship.

Subsection 3.1: Vulnerability:

Receiving love requires vulnerability, the willingness to open ourselves up to another person's affection and care. It means shedding the armor we've built around ourselves and allowing our partner to witness our true thoughts and emotions. By embracing vulnerability, we acknowledge and validate our partner's love, creating a safe space for emotional intimacy to flourish.

Subsection 3.2: Letting Go of Control:

Accepting love often requires relinquishing control and trusting our partner to meet our emotional needs. Allowing ourselves to depend on another person may seem daunting, but it fosters a sense of interdependence and mutual support within the relationship. By letting go of control, we grant our partner the opportunity to demonstrate their love and nurturing instincts.

Subsection 3.3: Gratitude:

Expressing gratitude for the love we receive fosters a positive cycle of love and affection within the relationship. By acknowledging and appreciating our partner's gestures of love, we encourage them to continue expressing their affection, reinforcing the deep bond between us. Gratitude begets love, creating an environment of warmth, appreciation, and mutual respect.

Section 4: Striking a Balance:

A harmonious relationship requires a delicate balance between giving and receiving love. It is essential to avoid an imbalance where one person consistently gives more than they receive, leading to emotional exhaustion and resentment. Open communication, setting healthy boundaries, and actively addressing needs and concerns ensure that both individuals feel loved and cared for.

Giving and receiving love in relationships is a continuous journey that evolves with time. It is through acts of love, both small and significant, that we create strong and thriving connections. By understanding the various methods of expressing love and embracing vulnerability, we foster a deep sense of intimacy and fulfillment within our relationships. Remember, love is not a finite resource; the more we give, the more we receive.

Chapter 6: Embracing Change and Growth

Change is an inevitable part of life. Whether we like it or not, we constantly find ourselves amidst a sea of changes, both big and small. From transitioning into a new phase of life to adapting to unforeseen circumstances, change surrounds us on a daily basis. In this chapter, we will explore the importance of embracing change and growth, and how these two interconnected concepts can empower us to lead fulfilling lives.

Understanding Change

To truly embrace change, we must first understand its nature. Change is the natural progression of events that shapes and molds us into who we are. It can take various forms - from shifts in our personal relationships to transformations in our professional endeavors. Change challenges us, pushes our limits, and forces us out of our comfort zones. It's in these transformative moments that we discover our true potential.

Change is not always easy. It often comes with uncertainty, disruption, and fear. We tend to resist it, clinging to the familiar and the secure. However, it is through embracing change that we grow and become the best versions of ourselves. When we resist change, we stagnate, remaining trapped in a limited perception of what is possible. But when we embrace change, we unlock doors to new opportunities, personal development, and self-discovery.

The Power of Growth

Embracing change is closely intertwined with the concept of growth. Growth is not simply about getting bigger or accumulating material possessions. True growth is the conscious effort to expand our knowledge, skills, and experiences, allowing us to evolve and flourish as individuals. It is about nurturing our minds, bodies, and souls.

Growth and change go hand in hand. When we embrace change, we open ourselves up to new experiences and ideas. This openness sets the stage for growth, enabling us to discover new passions, acquire new skills, and develop a broader perspective of the world around us. Growth nurtures our intellectual, emotional, and spiritual well-being, creating a solid foundation upon which change can take root and flourish.

Navigating the Winds of Change

Now that we understand the significance of change and growth, let's explore some strategies to help us navigate the often tumultuous waters of change.

1. Embrace Uncertainty: Change often brings with it a sense of uncertainty. Instead of fearing the unknown, embrace it with curiosity and an open mind. This attitude will enable you to adapt more easily and seize the opportunities that come your way.

2. Cultivate Resilience: Change can be challenging, but resilience is your secret weapon. Cultivate resilience by focusing on building a strong support network, practicing self-care, and maintaining a positive mindset. With resilience, you can weather any storm and come out stronger on the other side.

3. Embrace Your Inner Explorer: Change is an adventure waiting to unfold. Approach it with the spirit of an explorer, ready to discover new territories within yourself. Embrace the challenges, take risks, and relish the journey, knowing that growth lies just beyond the horizon.

4. Continual Learning and Adaptation: Embracing change goes hand in hand with continual learning and adaptation. Stay curious, seek out new knowledge, and be adaptable in your approach. This mindset will enable you to stay ahead of the curve and navigate the ever-changing landscape of life.

Overcoming Resistance to Change

While change is necessary for growth, we often find ourselves resistant to it. There are several reasons why we resist change, including fear of the unknown, fear of failure, and the comfort of familiarity. However, by identifying and addressing these resistance factors head-on, we can learn to embrace change more effectively.

1. Acknowledge Your Fear: Fear is a natural response to change. Instead of burying it or denying its existence, acknowledge your fears and allow yourself to feel them. Once you acknowledge your fears, you can begin to address them and move forward.

2. Challenge Your Beliefs: Often, our resistance to change stems from deeply ingrained beliefs and assumptions. Challenge these beliefs and question their validity. Are they serving you or limiting your growth? By challenging beliefs, you open yourself up to new possibilities and perspectives.

3. Take Small Steps: Change can be overwhelming, especially when we view it as a massive leap instead of a series of manageable steps. Break down change into smaller, more attainable goals. Celebrate each milestone along the way, building momentum as you progress.

Embracing Personal Growth

Embracing change and growth is a deeply personal journey. It requires self-reflection, self-awareness, and a commitment to continuous improvement. Here are some key areas to focus on when embarking on your personal growth journey.

1. Emotional Intelligence: Develop your emotional intelligence by becoming more aware of your emotions, managing them effectively, and empathizing with others. Emotional intelligence enhances your ability to navigate change and build meaningful relationships.

2. Self-Reflection: Set aside time for self-reflection. Consider your values, goals, and dreams. Reflecting upon your experiences and actions enables you to evaluate your growth and make necessary adjustments for future development.

3. Cultivate Positivity: Positive thinking is a powerful tool for personal growth. Surround yourself with positive influences, practice gratitude, and cultivate a growth mindset. By shifting your perspective towards positivity, you foster an environment that nurtures growth and change.

Embracing change and growth is not always easy, but it is necessary for personal development and fulfillment. Change challenges us to become better versions of ourselves. By understanding the nature of change, cultivating resilience, and embracing our inner explorers, we can navigate the winds of change with grace and purpose. Overcoming resistance to change requires acknowledging our fears, challenging our beliefs, and taking small, actionable steps. Finally, embracing personal growth involves developing emotional intelligence, engaging in self-reflection, and cultivating positivity.

Embracing Change as a Catalyst for Growth

Change is an inevitable part of life. We live in a world that is constantly evolving, and whether we like it or not, we must adapt to the shifting tides of time. In this chapter, we explore the concept of embracing change as a catalyst for growth. We delve into the significance of embracing change, the barriers that hinder our acceptance, and strategies to overcome them. By the end of this chapter, we hope to empower you with the tools to navigate change with confidence, enabling personal and professional growth.

The Importance of Embracing Change:

Change is often seen as daunting and disruptive, causing unease and uncertainty. However, it is crucial to understand that change is a necessary ingredient for growth. When we resist change, we become stagnant, limiting our potential for improvement. Embracing change allows us to expand our horizons, challenge our comfort zones, and discover new opportunities. We step into the realm of possibilities, enabling us to realize our full potential.

Embracing change also fosters resilience, which is vital in an ever-changing world. By adapting to change, we develop the ability to bounce back from setbacks more efficiently. Resilience allows us to face challenges head-on, embrace uncertainty, and overcome obstacles with determination. Thus, embracing change not only leads to personal and professional growth but also equips us with the strength to face future challenges.

Barriers to Embracing Change:

Despite the numerous benefits of embracing change, many individuals struggle to do so due to various barriers. These barriers may include fear of the unknown, comfort in routine, or attachment to the past. To truly embrace change, we must identify and understand these barriers, finding ways to overcome them.

Fear of the unknown is a common barrier to embracing change. Change often carries uncertainty, which can trigger anxiety and resistance. We naturally crave stability, as it provides us with a sense of security. However, it is important to acknowledge that growth lies beyond our comfort zones. To overcome the fear of the unknown, we must shift our mindset, viewing change as an opportunity for growth rather than a threat. By reframing our perception, we can navigate change with confidence and curiosity.

Comfort in routine is another barrier that hinders our ability to embrace change. We become accustomed to our habits and ways of doing things, creating a sense of familiarity. Stepping into the unknown may disrupt this familiarity, making us apprehensive. However, it is essential to recognize that growth requires us to break free from our comfort zones. Embracing change allows us to expand our horizons, gain new perspectives, and enhance our skill sets. By acknowledging the benefits of change, we can overcome the comfort of routine and open ourselves to new possibilities.

Attachment to the past is often a significant hindrance when faced with change. We hold onto memories, experiences, and relationships that have shaped us. While it is essential to honor our past, clinging to it too tightly can limit our growth. It is essential to let go of the past, allowing ourselves to evolve and embrace the present. By acknowledging that the only constant in life is change, we can release our attachment to the past and open ourselves up to new beginnings.

Strategies for Embracing Change:

Overcoming barriers to change may seem like an arduous task, but with the right strategies, it becomes more attainable. Here, we explore some effective techniques to help you embrace change and catalyze growth in your personal and professional life.

1. Shifting Perspective: Begin by altering your mindset towards change. Instead of perceiving it as a threat, see it as an opportunity for growth. View change as a chance to learn, evolve, and become a

better version of yourself. By changing your perspective, you reframe your perception and approach change with a positive mindset.

2. Cultivate Resilience: Embracing change requires resilience. Cultivate resilience by building a strong support network, practicing self-care, and nurturing a growth mindset. Surround yourself with individuals who inspire and motivate you, engage in activities that rejuvenate your spirit, and foster a belief that challenges are stepping stones to growth.

3. Flexibility and Adaptability: Develop a flexible and adaptable mindset that embraces change as a natural part of life. Embrace uncertainty and approach change with a sense of curiosity, as it provides opportunities for innovation and growth. Stay open-minded, continually learning, and seeking new knowledge. Flexibility and adaptability are key in navigating change with ease.

4. Set Goals and Take Action: Setting clear goals provides a sense of direction and purpose. When faced with change, identify what you aim to achieve and create actionable steps towards your objectives. By taking proactive steps, you regain a sense of control and empower yourself to embrace change.

5. Embrace Continuous Learning: Change often requires acquiring new skills and knowledge. Embrace the idea of lifelong learning, both

personally and professionally. Seek opportunities for growth, such as attending workshops, signing up for courses, or reading books. Embracing continuous learning allows you to adapt to change more effectively and thrive in ever-evolving environments.

In this chapter, we explored the concept of embracing change as a catalyst for growth. We discussed the importance of embracing change and the barriers that hinder our acceptance.

By shifting our perspective, cultivating resilience, and developing flexibility, we can overcome these barriers and embrace change effectively.

Embracing change opens doors to new opportunities, enhances personal and professional growth, and empowers us with resilience.

As we journey through life, let us remember that change is not to be feared but embraced as a transformative force leading us towards growth and fulfillment.

Adapting to Life Transitions with Grace

Life is a continuous journey marked by numerous transitions. Some transitions, whether big or small, are inevitable and thrust upon us, while others are by choice. Regardless of their origin, life transitions have the power to shape us and propel us towards personal growth and transformation. Adapting to these transitions with grace can be a challenging task, but one that is crucial for leading a fulfilling and meaningful life. In this chapter, we will explore the art of embracing life transitions with poise, resilience, and a positive mindset.

Understanding Life Transitions

Life transitions come in various forms and can occur in any area of our lives, such as career, relationships, health, or personal development. They encompass pivotal moments that require us to let go of the familiar and move forward into the unknown. Some common transitions include starting a new job, moving to a different city or country, getting married, becoming a parent, experiencing the loss of a loved one, or retiring from a long-held profession. What makes life transitions so formidable is the combination of uncertainty, unpredictability, and potential loss they bring. This cocktail of emotions can leave us feeling overwhelmed, anxious, and resistant to change. However, by adopting a proactive and open-minded approach, we can navigate these transitions with grace.

Embracing The Power of Mindset

The foundation of adapting to life transitions with grace lies in cultivating the right mindset. Our perception of these transitions greatly influences our experience and ability to adapt. Instead of viewing transitions as threats, we can choose to see them as opportunities for growth and self-discovery. This shift in perspective allows us to let go of fear and embrace the possibilities that lie ahead. Developing a growth mindset is essential during times of transition. This mindset, coined by renowned psychologist Carol Dweck, is characterized by a belief that our abilities can improve with effort and learning. By adopting a growth mindset, we increase our resilience and ability to adapt, as we recognize that transitions offer us valuable lessons and chances for personal development. Embracing the power of mindset helps us approach life transitions with curiosity, optimism, and a determination to make the most of the challenges that lie ahead.

Navigating the Emotional Landscape

Life transitions can bring about a rollercoaster of emotions. Acknowledging and navigating the emotional landscape that accompanies these transitions is vital to adapting with grace. One of the most common emotions experienced during transitions is grief.

Even positive transitions, such as getting married or starting a new job, can trigger grief for the life we are leaving behind. Recognizing and honoring this grief allows us to process it and provide ourselves with the necessary emotional support.

Another common emotion experienced during transitions is fear. Fear stems from the uncertainty and potential loss associated with the unknown. To manage fear, it is essential to cultivate self-compassion and develop strategies that promote self-care and emotional well-being. Engaging in mindfulness practices, seeking support from loved ones, and engaging in activities that bring joy and fulfillment can help us navigate and overcome fear during life transitions.

Building a Support System

The power of having a support system during life transitions cannot be overstated. Surrounding ourselves with individuals who uplift and encourage us is crucial in maintaining a positive and graceful approach. A support system can consist of friends, family, mentors, or even professional coaches who provide guidance and perspective during times of change.

In addition to seeking support from others, it is equally important to be self-reliant and develop a strong sense of self. Building resilience and fostering self-belief allows us to adapt to life transitions with grace, even if our support system is temporarily unavailable. Cultivating self-awareness, practicing self-care, and setting clear intentions are powerful tools for developing self-reliance and inner strength.

Embracing Flexibility and Adaptability

Adapting to life transitions requires flexibility and adaptability, as we navigate new territories and adjust to unfamiliar circumstances. Resistance to change can hinder our ability to adapt gracefully. Instead, we must develop a willingness to embrace the unknown and be open to new possibilities.

Embracing flexibility also means relinquishing control over things beyond our reach. Life transitions often come with a lack of certainty and definitive outcomes. By surrendering the need to control every aspect, we free ourselves from unnecessary stress and anxiety. This surrender allows us to flow with the changes, rather than against them, and cultivate a sense of ease and grace throughout the transition process.

Adapting to life transitions with grace is an art that can be mastered with practice, self-reflection, and a positive mindset. By understanding the nature of life transitions, embracing the power of mindset, navigating emotions, building a support system, and embracing flexibility, we can embark on new chapters of our lives with confidence and serenity. Life transitions offer endless possibilities for growth and personal development, should we choose to approach them with grace. So, let us be open to the journey ahead, knowing that embracing transitions is not only essential but also an opportunity to evolve into the best versions of ourselves.

Learning from Setbacks and Failures

In the journey of life, setbacks and failures are inevitable companions. Whether we like it or not, they will find their way into our lives, challenging us, testing our resilience, and putting our dreams to the ultimate test. However, it is important to remember that setbacks and failures are not the end; instead, they can serve as valuable teachers that guide us toward personal growth and achievement. It is through these challenging moments that we realize our weaknesses and discover the true strength that lies within us. In this chapter, we will explore the power of learning from setbacks and failures and how they can shape our lives and lead us toward success.

Section 1: Embracing Failure as a Stepping Stone to Success

It is a universal truth that everyone, without exception, experiences failure at some point in their lives. The key lies in how we perceive and react to these failures. Rather than viewing them as permanent roadblocks, we must embrace them as stepping stones that propel us toward our goals. It is through failure that we learn valuable lessons about ourselves, our abilities, and our limitations.

One prominent example of embracing failure is the story of Thomas

Edison, the inventor of the light bulb. Edison experienced numerous setbacks during his quest to create a functioning light bulb. However, instead of becoming discouraged by failure, he famously remarked, "I have not failed. I've just found 10,000 ways that won't work." Edison understood that failure was merely a part of the journey towards success. By embracing his setbacks, he was ultimately able to revolutionize the world through his invention.

Section 2: Learn, Adapt, and Overcome

When setbacks occur, it is crucial to take a step back and assess the situation. Rather than dwelling on what went wrong, we should focus on what can be learned from the experience. Failure offers valuable insights that cannot be gained through success alone. It forces us to question our approach, evaluate our strategies, and make necessary improvements.

An example of learning, adapting, and overcoming can be found in the world of sports. Consider the story of Michael Jordan, widely regarded as one of the greatest basketball players of all time. Jordan faced numerous failures and setbacks throughout his career, including being cut from his high school basketball team. Instead of letting this setback define him, Jordan used it as motivation to improve his skills and prove his worth. He later said, "I've missed more than 9,000 shots in my career. I've lost almost 300 games. Twenty-six times, I've been trusted to take the game-winning shot and missed. I've failed over and over and over again in my life. And that is why I succeed." Jordan's ability to learn from his failures and adapt his approach ultimately led him to achieve unparalleled success in his sport.

Section 3: Building Resilience through Failure

Setbacks and failures can be disheartening, leaving us feeling defeated and unsure of our capabilities. However, it is important to view these challenges as opportunities to develop resilience. Resilience is the ability to bounce back from adversity stronger than before. It is a skill that can be cultivated through facing and overcoming failure.

The story of J.K. Rowling, the author of the beloved Harry Potter series, serves as a testament to the power of resilience. Before achieving literary fame, Rowling faced numerous failures and setbacks, including divorce, poverty, and rejection from multiple publishers. However, she refused to give up on her dream. Rowling channeled her setbacks into determination, resilience, and unwavering faith in her abilities. Her resilience paid off, and today she is one of the most successful authors of all time.

Section 4: Cultivating Growth Mindset: The Key to Success

One crucial mindset in the face of setbacks and failures is the adoption of a growth mindset. Developed by psychologist Carol Dweck, a growth mindset believes that intelligence and abilities are not fixed but can be developed through dedication, hard work, and learning from failure. Cultivating a growth mindset empowers us to view setbacks as opportunities for growth and self-improvement.

Consider the story of Elon Musk, the visionary entrepreneur behind companies such as Tesla and SpaceX. Throughout his career, Musk has faced numerous setbacks, including multiple rocket failures and the brink of bankruptcy. Despite these challenges, he maintains a growth mindset, constantly learning from his mistakes, adapting his strategies, and pushing through failure. Musk's relentless pursuit of growth and innovation has propelled him to become one of the most influential figures of our time.

Section 5: Learning from setbacks and failures is an essential aspect of personal development and growth. By embracing failure as a stepping stone, learning from our experiences, adapting our strategies, building resilience, and cultivating a growth mindset, we can transform setbacks into opportunities for success. We must remember that setbacks and failures are not indicators of our worth or abilities; rather, they are necessary teachers that guide us toward achieving our true potential. As we navigate through life's challenges, let us embrace setbacks and failures, for they hold the keys to unlock our untapped potential and pave the way toward a brighter future.

Evolving and Becoming Your Best Self

"The only constant in life is change." We've all heard this quote at some point in our lives, and yet, it holds so much truth. As humans, we are constantly evolving, growing, and striving to become better versions of ourselves. The journey towards self-improvement is not a one-time event but rather a lifelong process filled with ups and downs, hopes and setbacks, triumphs and failures. In this chapter, we will explore the different aspects of evolving and becoming your best self, sharing insights, tips, and personal anecdotes to inspire and guide you on this transformative journey.

Understanding the Process of Evolution

To embark on a journey of self-improvement, it is crucial to understand the process of evolution. Evolution is not merely a physical concept but includes emotional, mental, and spiritual growth as well. It involves an internal drive to better oneself, to break free from old patterns and limitations, and to embrace change and personal development.

At its core, the process of evolution involves self-awareness. This means becoming deeply acquainted with your emotions, behaviors, strengths, and weaknesses. Self-awareness allows you to identify areas for improvement, set goals, and create a roadmap to becoming your best self. It requires embracing vulnerability, being honest with yourself, and accepting that growth often requires stepping out of your comfort zone.

Embracing Change and Overcoming Resistance

As we embark on our journey towards self-improvement, it is vital to acknowledge that change can be uncomfortable. We often resist change due to fear, uncertainty, or the desire to stay within familiar territory. However, true growth embraces change and challenges us to break free from our self-imposed limitations.

To overcome resistance to change, it is essential to cultivate a growth mindset. A growth mindset encourages us to view challenges as opportunities for growth rather than obstacles to our success. It enables us to learn from our failures, persevere through setbacks, and see potential in every situation.

Self-reflection and Goal Setting

Self-reflection is a powerful tool for personal growth. Taking the time to reflect on our thoughts, actions, and experiences allows us to recognize patterns, identify areas for improvement, and discover our true passions and values. Through self-reflection, we can make informed decisions that align with our authentic selves.

Goal setting is an integral part of personal evolution. Setting clear and realistic goals provides us with a sense of direction and purpose, motivating us to strive for our best selves. When setting goals, it is crucial to make them specific, measurable, attainable, relevant, and time-bound (SMART). By breaking down our goals into smaller, actionable steps, we make our journey towards self-improvement more manageable and achievable.

Developing Empathy and Building Emotional Intelligence

Becoming our best selves goes beyond personal achievements; it also involves our relationships with others. Developing empathy and emotional intelligence are vital skills that help us navigate social interactions, foster connections, and create a positive impact on the world around us.

Empathy is the ability to understand and share the feelings of another. It requires actively listening, stepping into someone else's shoes, and withholding judgment. By practicing empathy, we can build deeper connections, resolve conflicts, and demonstrate compassion towards others.

Emotional intelligence is the ability to recognize, understand, and manage our own emotions, as well as the emotions of others. It involves being aware of our emotional states, regulating our emotions effectively, and empathetically responding to others' emotions. Developing emotional intelligence helps us make better decisions, build stronger relationships, and navigate life's challenges with grace and resilience.

Cultivating Self-care and Well-being

To become our best selves, we must prioritize self-care and well-being. Taking care of our physical, mental, and emotional health ensures we have the energy, clarity, and resilience to pursue personal growth and make a positive impact on our lives and the lives of others.

Self-care encompasses a wide range of practices, from physical exercise and healthy eating to meditation, journaling, and engaging in hobbies that bring us joy. It involves setting boundaries, learning to say no when necessary, and prioritizing activities that nourish our mind, body, and soul.

Maintaining a Growth Mindset and Embracing Lifelong Learning

Lastly, the journey towards becoming our best selves requires us to maintain a growth mindset and embrace lifelong learning. A growth mindset allows us to view every experience as an opportunity to learn, grow, and improve. It encourages us to seek new knowledge, challenge our beliefs, and continuously adapt in an ever-changing world.

Embracing lifelong learning involves actively seeking out new experiences, acquiring new skills, and broadening our perspectives. It encourages us to step outside our comfort zones, take risks, and be open to new possibilities. By embracing a mindset of continuous learning, we engage in personal and intellectual growth, expanding our horizons and becoming more resilient and adaptable individuals.

In The journey towards becoming our best selves is an ongoing and ever-evolving process. It requires self-awareness, embracing change, setting goals, developing empathy and emotional intelligence, prioritizing self-care, and maintaining a growth mindset. It is through this transformative journey that we can unlock our full potential, create a meaningful life, and make a positive impact on ourselves and those around us. Remember, the only constant in life is change, and it is within that change that we find opportunities for growth, evolution, and becoming our best selves.

Expressing Yourself Authentically

In today's highly interconnected world, where conformity often takes center stage, expressing oneself authentically has become a rare and precious trait. Human beings have an inherent desire to be understood, acknowledged, and appreciated for who they truly are. However, societal pressures and the fear of judgment and rejection often mask our true selves, preventing us from embracing our individuality fully.

In this chapter, we will delve deep into the power of expressing yourself authentically, unraveling its significance, benefits, and the various obstacles that may hinder this self-expression journey. Through inspiring stories, practical tips, and insightful exercises, we aim to help you embrace your unique voice, nurture your self-confidence, and unlock the immense potential that lies within.

Understanding Self-Expression:

Authentic self-expression is the ability to communicate your thoughts, emotions, and values honestly and openly, without fear of judgment or rejection. It involves aligning your external expression with your internal feelings, allowing your true self to shine through every interaction and situation.

One key aspect of authentic self-expression is developing self-awareness. By understanding our values, beliefs, and emotions, we can cultivate a sense of authenticity that resonates with ourselves and others. When we express ourselves without pretense or artifice, we build genuine connections and foster deep relationships based on trust and understanding.

The Benefits of Authentic Self-Expression:

Embracing authentic self-expression can have numerous positive effects on our lives. When we express ourselves authentically, we invite others to do the same, creating an environment that encourages openness and vulnerability. This, in turn, leads to enhanced communication, collaboration, and teamwork in personal and professional relationships.

Authentic self-expression also nurtures self-confidence and self-acceptance. By embracing our unique qualities and showcasing them to the world, we acknowledge our worthiness and build resilience against external judgments. This self-assurance allows us to pursue our passions, take risks, and embrace opportunities that align with our true selves, leading to a more fulfilling and purposeful life.

Obstacles to Authentic Self-Expression:

While expressing oneself authentically is undoubtedly a powerful endeavor, it is not without its challenges. Society's pressure to conform, fear of judgment, and past experiences of rejection can create barriers that impede our ability to express ourselves openly and honestly.

Additionally, our own internal narratives and self-limiting beliefs can hinder our authentic self-expression. We may question whether our thoughts and feelings are valid or worthy of being shared, leading to self-censorship and a loss of our true voice. In order to overcome these obstacles, we must actively work on dismantling these barriers, cultivating self-compassion, and embracing vulnerability as a strength rather than a weakness.

Cultivating Authentic Self-Expression:

To begin the journey of expressing yourself authentically, it is crucial to nurture self-acceptance and self-compassion. Understand that you are worthy and deserving of expressing yourself honestly, regardless of societal expectations or past experiences. Practice treating yourself with kindness, and grant yourself permission to embrace your uniqueness without seeking validation from others.

Developing self-awareness is another essential element in cultivating authentic self-expression. Take time to reflect on your values, beliefs, and desires. By understanding yourself on a deeper level, you can align your external actions and expressions with your internal truth.

It is also important to surround yourself with supportive individuals who appreciate and celebrate your authentic self. Seek out environments and communities where you feel accepted and valued for who you truly are. These connections will provide the encouragement and validation needed to express yourself authentically.

Practical Exercises and Techniques:

Throughout this chapter, we will guide you through various exercises and techniques to enhance your authentic self-expression. These exercises aim to help you connect with your emotions, challenge self-limiting beliefs, and build resilience against external judgments.

One powerful technique that can facilitate authentic self-expression is journaling. Set aside dedicated time each day to write freely and honestly about your thoughts and emotions. This practice will not only increase self-awareness but also serve as a platform to process and release any emotions that may be holding you back.

Another useful exercise is engaging in creative expressions such as painting, music, or dance. These outlets provide a non-verbal way to express your emotions and creativity, allowing your authentic self to shine through without the confines of words.

Furthermore, practicing active listening and empathy towards others fosters a safe and supportive environment for authentic self-expression. By actively engaging in conversation, suspending judgment, and seeking to understand others, we create a space where everyone feels comfortable being themselves.

Expressing yourself authentically is a transformative journey that requires self-awareness, self-acceptance, and resilience. By embracing your uniqueness, nurturing self-confidence, and dismantling societal barriers, you can develop the courage to express yourself honestly and openly.

Through the exercises, techniques, and insights shared in this chapter, we hope to empower you to unleash your true voice and connect with others on a deeper, more meaningful level. Remember, authentic self-expression is not just a personal endeavor; it is a transformative power that can inspire and uplift those around you, creating a ripple effect of authenticity and connection throughout the world.

Honoring Your Voice and Opinions

In a world filled with diverse perspectives, it is crucial to recognize the importance of honoring your own voice and opinions. Each and every one of us possesses a unique set of experiences, beliefs, and thoughts that shape our individuality. Yet, many people often find themselves hesitating to express their true selves, fearing judgment or invalidation by others. This chapter aims to explore the significance of honoring your voice and opinions, empowering you to embrace your authenticity, and fostering meaningful connections with others.

Unveiling the Power of Your Voice:

Your voice is more than just the sounds that leave your lips; it is a reflection of your inner self. Each word you speak carries the potential to inspire, inform, and challenge those around you. Nevertheless, many individuals remain silent, doubting the worthiness of their contributions. It is imperative to understand that your voice holds an inherent value, regardless of external validation.

To honor your voice, it is critical to cultivate self-acceptance. Embrace your uniqueness and acknowledge that your thoughts and opinions are valid, regardless of their alignment with societal norms.

Trust in your ability to contribute to conversations, share your ideas, and influence change.

Discovering the Courage Within:

Honoring your voice requires courage, as it often entails stepping outside your comfort zone. However, true growth and self-discovery transpire when you have the audacity to rise above the fear of judgment and express your truth. Understandably, this is no small feat, but it is an essential step towards personal empowerment.

Take a moment to reflect on your core values and beliefs. What do you stand for? What ideas do you wish to champion? Once you identify these principles, you can start mustering the courage necessary to voice them. Remember, courage is not the absence of fear; rather, it is the ability to press forward despite it. Embrace discomfort as a catalyst for growth and challenge yourself to honor your voice even in the face of adversity.

Navigating Obstacles and Challenges:

Throughout your journey to honor your voice and opinions, you may encounter various obstacles and challenges. It is important to recognize these hurdles not as insurmountable roadblocks, but as opportunities for growth and learning.

One of the most common challenges is the fear of judgment. When you express your opinions, not everyone will agree or appreciate your perspective. However, learning to be comfortable with dissent is a crucial part of personal growth. It allows you to develop resilience, expand your understanding of different viewpoints, and engage in meaningful dialogues.

Additionally, societal conditioning often discourages individuals from expressing opinions that do not align with the mainstream narrative. Many fear being labeled as "different" or "rebellious." Transcending these biases requires an unwavering belief in the value of your voice and a commitment to authenticity. Remember, society progresses when individuals dare to challenge the status quo and share their unique insights.

Building Meaningful Connections:

Honoring your voice and opinions not only empowers you as an individual but also facilitates the establishment of deep, meaningful connections with others. When you truly embrace your authenticity and express your thoughts openly, you create fertile ground for genuine conversations and mutual understanding.

However, it is crucial to remember that honoring your voice does not equate to dismissing or disrespecting the opinions of others. True empowerment lies in embracing the diversity of perspectives that exist in the world. Engage in discussions with an open heart and mind, seeking to understand and appreciate the experiences that shape the viewpoints of those around you. Remember that meaningful connections are built on a foundation of respect and empathy.

Furthermore, actively seek out spaces that encourage open dialogue, where your voice is heard and valued. Surrounding yourself with individuals who appreciate and respect your opinions will not only bolster your self-confidence but also challenge and inspire you to evolve intellectually.

Honoring your voice and opinions is a lifelong journey, fueled by self-acceptance, courage, and a commitment to growth. By embracing your authentic self, you unlock the transformative power of your voice, becoming a catalyst for change and personal empowerment. However, this journey is rarely devoid of obstacles, and it is essential to confront them with resilience and an open mind.

Remember, your voice is unique and invaluable. It serves as a vehicle to express your truths, contribute to the world, and foster genuine connections with others. Take a stand, honor your voice, and let it resonate boldly within you.

Creativity as a Form of Self-Expression

In the realm of human existence, creativity is a force that is inherent within each and every one of us. It transcends boundaries and emerges in various forms, allowing individuals to express themselves uniquely. From painting and music to writing and dance, creativity has the power to weave together the fabric of our soul, enabling us to connect with ourselves and the world around us on a deeper level. In this chapter, we will explore the intricate relationship between creativity and self-expression—how the act of creating grants us a means of unveiling our innermost thoughts, emotions, and desires. Through our exploration, we will discover the transformative nature of creativity and how it serves as a gateway to self-discovery and authenticity.

The Art of Self-Expression:

Throughout history, humans have sought opportunities for self-expression, finding solace in creatively expressing their inner thoughts, beliefs, and experiences. Whether it be through a vibrant painting or a haunting melody, art provides individuals with an outlet to communicate the depths of their being. Renowned artist Pablo Picasso once said, "Every artist dips his brush in his own soul and paints his own nature into his pictures." This statement exemplifies the idea that creativity is a manifestation of the artist's inner world, allowing their true essence to be unveiled through their art form.

When an individual engages in creative expression, they delve into a realm beyond the limits of verbal communication. Words, while powerful mediums themselves, often fall short in capturing the complexity of human experience. However, the expression of one's self through art transcends the confines of language, enabling us to convey emotions, experiences, and ideas that are otherwise indescribable.

The Catharsis of Creation:

Creative expression serves as a profound catharsis, allowing individuals to release deep-seated emotions that may otherwise remain dormant within their psyche. Art offers a safe space for exploring the depths of our consciousness, providing an avenue for the release, exploration, and understanding of the complexities of human emotions. By channeling our innermost thoughts and feelings into our creative endeavors, we find relief, solace, and even healing.

In the process of creating, we are continually confronted with our authentic selves—our fears, desires, vulnerabilities, and strengths. This self-confrontation not only leads to self-exploration but also allows us to overcome personal barriers and limitations. As we create, we are compelled to challenge our comfort zones, push boundaries, and embrace the unknown, fostering personal growth and self-discovery.

The Spark of Imagination:

At the heart of creativity lies the power of imagination—an intrinsic human quality that enables us to envision possibilities beyond our current reality. Imagination is the catalyst that drives us to explore and experiment with various artistic forms. It ignites a spark of inspiration within us, pushing us to seek novel ways of expressing our innermost selves.

Through the act of creation, we tap into the infinite well of imagination, allowing our visions and ideas to materialize in tangible forms. It is through this process that we give birth to original thoughts, concepts, and innovations that have the potential to shape our world. As Albert Einstein once said, "Imagination is more important than knowledge. For knowledge is limited, whereas imagination embraces the entire world, stimulating progress, giving birth to evolution."

Overcoming Resistance:

Although creativity has the potential to be a liberating force, many individuals find themselves battling resistance when endeavoring to express themselves. This resistance stems from fear—fear of judgment, rejection, or inadequacy—which can hinder the journey of self-expression. Society often imposes certain standards and expectations, creating a sense of self-doubt and discouraging individuals from fully embracing their creative instincts.

However, it is essential to recognize that creativity knows no bounds and thrives in freedom. As artist Georgia O'Keeffe once expressed, "I found I could say things with colors and shapes that I couldn't say any other way—things I had no words for." By embracing creativity, we liberate ourselves from the shackles of conformity and societal constraints, allowing our unique voice to soar freely.

With each brushstroke or pen stroke, each dance move or musical note, we have the opportunity to rebel against these inhibitions and express our true selves. In doing so, we not only empower ourselves but also inspire others to embark on their own creative journeys. Creativity, as a form of self-expression, serves as an essential cornerstone of the human spirit. It enables us to divulge our deepest thoughts, emotions, and desires, creating a bridge between our inner world and the external reality. Through the process of creation, we find catharsis, self-discovery, and personal growth, transforming our beings in profound ways.

As we embrace our creative instincts and allow our imagination to flourish, we dismantle the barriers that hinder our journey of self-expression. We become conduits through which our true selves are unveiled, leaving an indelible mark on the tapestry of human existence.

May we honor and celebrate the creativity within us, for it is a soulful testament to our authentic selves—the vibrant hues that color the canvas of our lives.